Success
International
English skills for IGCSE

Teacher's Book

Marian Barry

GEORGIAN PRESS

Georgian Press (Jersey) Limited
8 Duhamel Place
St Helier
Jersey JE1 3WF
Channel Islands

First published by Georgian Press (Jersey) Limited 1998

ISBN 1-873630-19-0

Produced by AMR Limited

Printed in Egypt by International Printing House

Contents

Student's Book Contents Chart

IGCSE IN ESL AT A GLANCE

Core curriculum

PAPER 1 Reading and Writing (1 ½ hours)
(Grades available: C – G)

PART 1: READING SKILLS

3 reading comprehension exercises based on brochures/adverts and newspaper/magazine texts. On average, there are 5 questions per exercise. Question formats are short-answer for exercise 1 with either short-answer or true-false/multiple-choice formats for exercises 2 and 3.

Skills required

Skim, scan and read closely to extract information. Incline of difficulty.

Total marks: 5 + 5 + 5 = 15

PART 2: INTEGRATED READING AND WRITING SKILLS

Exercise 1: Detailed comprehension text which may include information (charts etc) presented visually. Candidates answer about 5 questions. Answers to be sentence-length.

Exercise 2: Summary in 100 words.

Exercise 3: Fill in a form based on a given scenario.

Skills required

Detailed reading comprehension, including ability to understand statistical/visual information (ex.1).

Ability to write concisely in summary form using own words (ex. 2).

Ability to interpret a scenario and transfer information to a form as if candidate is the person in the scenario (ex. 3).

Total marks: 6 + 8 + 6 = 20

PART 3: WRITING SKILLS

2 composition questions.

Exercise 1 often has a visual stimulus (e.g. photos, picture, leaflet). Requires 100 words.

Exercise 2 may have a visual or verbal stimulus. Requires 150 words.

Contexts: formal/informal letters, articles for school newsletter/teenage magazine/newspaper.

Skills required

Write in connected prose, paragraph, punctuate, spell common words, use suitable tone/register, show audience awareness.

Total marks: 9 + 12 = 21

Total marks for Paper 1: 56
Weighting: 70%

Extended curriculum

PAPER 2 Reading and Writing (2 hours)
(Grades available: A – E)

PART 1: READING SKILLS

3 reading comprehension exercises based on brochures/adverts and newspaper/magazine texts. On average, there are 6 questions per exercise. Question formats are short-answer for exercise 1 with either short-answer or true-false/multiple-choice formats for exercises 2 and 3.

Overlap with Core

Texts for exercises 1 and 3 are the same. Questions are generally similar, with one or two more challenging questions added.

Exercise 2 is different.

Skills required

Skim, scan and read closely to extract information. Incline of difficulty.

Total marks: 7 + 5 + 6 = 18

PART 2: INTEGRATED READING AND WRITING SKILLS

Exercise 1: Detailed comprehension text which may include information (charts etc) presented visually. Candidates answer about 6 questions, the last of which requires a summary of about 60 words. Other answers to be sentence-length.

Exercise 2 : Summary in 100 words.

Exercise 3 : Either a further summary in 100 words or a note-taking exercise.

Overlap with Core

Text for exercise 1 is the same, but Core candidates are not asked to produce the 60-word summary to round off the task.

Exercise 2 is the same.

Exercise 3 is different (Core candidates fill in a form).

Skills required

Detailed reading comprehension, including ability to understand statistical/visual information and produce a brief summary (ex. 1).

Ability to write concisely in summary form using own words (ex. 2).

Ability to write a further summary or take a clear set of notes on a text (ex. 3).

Total marks: 10 + 8 + 8 = 26

PART 3: WRITING SKILLS

3 composition questions.

Exercise 1 often has a visual stimulus (e.g. photos, picture, leaflet). Requires 150 words.

Exercise 2 may have a visual or verbal stimulus. Requires 200 words.

Exercise 3 asks for arguments, opinions and views and the stimulus is usually verbal. Requires 150-200 words. Candidates often have to select from prompts.

Contexts: formal/informal letters, articles for school newsletter/teenage magazine/newspaper.

Overlap with Core

Exercises 1 and 2 have the same stimulus, but the word length is greater.

Skills required

Write in connected prose, paragraph, punctuate, spell words accurately, use varied vocabulary, present an argument, use suitable tone/register, show audience awareness.

Total marks: 12 + 16 + 12 = 40

Total marks for Paper 2: 84
Weighting: 70%

Core curriculum

PAPER 3 Listening   (30 minutes)

(Grades available: C - G)

PART 1: SIX BRIEF SCENARIOS

6 questions about information given in 6 very short, straightforward monologues/conversations.

Skills required

Identify one specific point of information for 5 questions. For one question, identify 2 specific points of information, e.g. a date and a time.

Total marks: 7

PART 2: TWO SHORT DIALOGUES/TALKS ETC

Candidates listen to 2 recordings (short formal talks, announcements, conversations etc) and fill in skeletal notes or close a gapped text with single words or short phrases.

Skills required

Pick out information from what may be incidental

Total marks: 12

PART 3: TWO LONGER TALKS/CONVERSATIONS ETC

Candidates listen to 2 recordings (informal conversations or more formal talks) and answer about 10 true-false or multiple-choice questions on each by ticking boxes. Each question is worth a half mark.

Skills required

Understand more complex meanings, views, opinions and attitudes of the speakers.

Total marks: 11

Total marks for Paper 3: 30
Weighting: 30%

Extended curriculum

PAPER 4 Listening   (45 minutes)

(Grades available: A - E)

PART 1: SIX BRIEF SCENARIOS

6 questions about information given in 6 very short, straightforward monologues/conversations.

Overlap with Core

3 scenarios and questions are the same, 3 are different and more complex.

Skills required

Identify one specific point of information for 4 questions. For 2 further questions, identify 2 specific points of information, e.g. name a place, give a reason.

Total marks: 8

PART 2: TWO SHORT DIALOGUES/TALKS ETC

Candidates listen to 2 recordings (short formal talks, announcements, conversations etc) and fill in skeletal notes.

Skills required

Pick out information from what may be incidental.

Overlap with Core

Recordings may be the same or they may be different. Candidates have to do more writing in their answers, e.g. complete notes more fully.

Total marks: 15

PART 3: TWO LONGER TALKS/CONVERSATIONS ETC

Candidates listen to 2 recordings (informal conversations or more formal talks) and answer about 6 short-answer questions on each.

Overlap with Core

One recording might be the same or it might be different. Core candidates have to tick boxes, and their questions are simpler.

Skills required

Understand more complex meanings, views, opinions and attitudes of the speakers.

Total marks: 13

Total marks for Paper 4: 36
Weighting: 30%

PAPER 5 (Core and Extended curriculum)
Oral Assessment   (15 minutes)

Candidates take part in a discussion with the examiner and possibly another candidate on a set topic. There are up to five topics. Typical topics, with prompts to guide the discussion, would be the rights and wrongs of zoos, holidays, winning the lottery, health and fitness, etc. Students respond to a range of questions posed by the examiner. The more able may also initiate discussion.

Extended candidates also have the option of 'Choose a topic', which has no guided prompts and requires more individual thought. There are five 'Choose a topic' questions to select from. These include controversial statements such as 'Money is the key to happiness' or 'Teachers should earn as much as film stars!'

Timing

The discussion lasts 15 minutes. The first few minutes are a warm-up phase which is not marked.

Skills

Candidates are marked on a grid covering communication, pronunciation, vocabulary, structures and flexibility. The best candidates can deal with abstract or intellectual concepts and communicate freely, but do not need to be of native speaker equivalence.

Marks

A mark range of 0-100 is available. Grades available range from 1 (highest) to 5 (lowest).

PAPER 6 (Core and Extended curriculum)
School-based Oral Assessment

This is a coursework option in which oral work is set and marked by the teacher. Prior agreement from UCLES should be sought if the coursework option is being considered.

Further information about the IGCSE in ESL can be obtained from:

IGCSE Office
University of Cambridge Local Examinations Syndicate
1 Hills Road
CAMBRIDGE CB1 2EU
United Kingdom

Introduction

Success International is a complete course, developed over several years, which provides detailed preparation for all the papers of the Cambridge IGCSE examination in English as a Second Language.

How the course reflects the exam

The course reflects the integrated skills basis of the exam. It takes a generic approach to skills, rather than treating individual skills as though they exist in watertight compartments. For example, a listening exercise is also exploited to develop topic and vocabulary knowledge, and to practise functional language and intonation.

The 'holistic' nature of the IGCSE in ESL derives from the expectation that candidates will be receiving their education through the medium of English, or be living in a country where English is widely spoken. Candidates will therefore be more used to and more comfortable with English than will 'pure' EFL candidates at a similar level. Unlike other language exams for non-native speakers, there is no isolated testing of freestanding structures.

As usage is integrated in the exam, the range of language candidates are expected to know is not made particularly explicit. Great care has therefore been taken in the course to break down and expose the layers of language structures and vocabulary, understanding of topics and concepts which are implicit in the IGCSE in ESL, without losing its integrated nature.

Educational aims and objectives

The course material is intended to be genuinely educational and to develop students both intellectually and linguistically, to increase personal awareness and to encourage international understanding. An investigative approach is taken, and students use initiative to solve problems. They apply skills, knowledge and understanding, and are encouraged to undertake individual projects and to work as part of a team. It is important that teachers develop these broader skills if the material is to work as intended. The educational aims and objectives of *Success International* also make it suitable for courses other than the IGCSE in ESL.

Age range

The course is designed to be used by young people in the age range 14-18. Unit themes reflect the interests of teenagers and aim to promote maturity of thought and outlook. This approach reflects the aims of the exam and the typical age range of candidates.

Time allocation

The course can be used over a period of up to two years, which is the recommended period of time suggested for the IGCSE in ESL curriculum. This takes into account young people's rate of intellectual and emotional development. Alternatively, the material can be adapted to be covered in one year if this is the time available. The progression of language work, and the selection and treatment of topics, have been carefully chosen to reflect these factors.

Ability range

The exam has a two-tier structure called Core and Extended which embraces a wide ability range, from lower-intermediate through to upper-intermediate. The material in the course covers all the aspects of the exam that Core and Extended students could be expected to meet. The emphasis is on the more challenging aspects of the exam, where candidates are failing to do themselves justice.

Course structure

The course is organised into ten topic-based units, each systematically and gradually developing the four skills. Exam-format listening and reading exercises are introduced early in the units and fully exploited. Oral work and writing skills are developed at various stages within a unit, but students are not expected to try exam-format writing or speaking assessment until the end of a unit, on the basis that these, the productive skills, are the most demanding. Teachers should encourage students to synthesise all that they have learned in terms of language acquisition and understanding of topics before expecting them to do exam-format writing and speaking tasks without help.

The units offer in-depth topic coverage, with shifts of focus clearly signposted by theme headings. By studying a topic from many angles, students will be better prepared for exam questions where new angles are set on familiar topics, and a certain depth of thought is rewarded.

Each unit has a number of regular features including structural work, vocabulary building, spelling, functions, model texts and an International Overview. The language study grows out of the texts that are being studied, to maximise relevance, accessibility and practical application.

Language study is also slanted to take account of IGCSE exam reports, which highlight those areas where improvements are needed, or where candidates have shown encouraging signs which should be further developed. These include: tone/register and audience awareness, vocabulary enlargement, understanding of topic, spelling, idioms and use of colloquial language, punctuation, paragraphing, and range of structures.

How to use the units

LEAD-IN

Each unit starts with a student-centred lead-in which introduces the topic and presents language and concepts. Students engage in stimulating group and pair work, in which they share experience and acquire new insights. Teachers should use the lead-in to expose and remedy knowledge gaps, e.g. key vocabulary needed for later work in the unit, before plunging deeper into the topic. The Teacher's notes always provide a full back-up to support the lead-in.

DEVELOPING READING SKILLS

Most units have two substantial reading texts from a variety of authentic sources, representing a wide range of styles but, as in the exam, staying within what teenagers could be expected to experience or imagine. Texts are chosen specifically to practise skills such as skimming, scanning and detailed reading as required by IGCSE.

Students are introduced to the reading texts through a range of structured exercises including speculation and prediction, and vocabulary and language checks. Texts are often enhanced by a visual image to help students focus fully on the topic. Teachers should make full use of the visual support to draw in weaker students. Some texts are accompanied by a checklist which students should refer to after reading to help them understand features inherent in textual organisation, such as paragraphing and argument development.

Follow-up exercises always start with comprehension to check understanding of information and lead on to detailed language study which has grown out of the text. The reading comprehension question format (short-answer/true-false/multiple-choice) and number of questions mirror the exam.

WRITING SKILLS

Writing skills receive particular treatment. The overall aim is to develop a more mature writing style which meets exam requirements for the highest marks whilst stimulating individuality of style and expression. A range of devices are employed which are suitable for use at different levels, so that teachers can involve the weaker students fully. These include working from models, comparing and contrasting typical IGCSE students' styles and approaches to writing tasks, completing notes, and reorganising texts. There is a special focus on the subtle areas of tone, register and audience awareness which repay detailed study. Many of the exercises are derived from previous IGCSE exam questions which have presented typical problems.

LISTENING SKILLS

There are ten recorded listening passages which reflect the exam formats and two 'model' conversations which students can listen to and read at the same time. Young voices have been used in a few of the recordings for greater authenticity. Listening passages range from recorded announcements to talks with a factual or opinion-based content. The question formats following the tasks reflect typical exam formats, e.g. true/false, short answer, etc.

Listening texts are multi-purpose. Not only do they build specific skills, such as listening for a specific

point or listening for attitude, they also demonstrate a range of linguistic strategies including functional language (interrupting, expressing disagreement, blaming) and phonological features (pronunciation, stress and intonation) which will be tested in the oral assessment.

SPEAKING

Oral work is encouraged at every opportunity, and through whole class interaction, pair work, reading aloud and so on. Structured oral exercises develop more understanding of functions, pronunciation, intonation and stress, giving talks effectively, responding to an audience and interacting with a speaker. The exercises will work at different levels and with more introverted students if teachers give credibility to oral work by making time for it in the classroom. The oral work leads up to exam-format oral assessment exercises at the end of the unit.

LANGUAGE STUDY AND GRAMMAR

The language study includes structural work, vocabulary, spelling, punctuation, paragraphing, and idiomatic and figurative language. The work is based on deductive reasoning, so teachers should build on students' prior knowledge and experience. Students should be encouraged to study the examples in the coursebook and to work out meaning, patterns, rules and exceptions. This principle should be applied whether students are working on spelling, grammar or punctuation, or building vocabulary.

The space given to grammar teaching in the course is balanced against the need to develop a range of skills, and the priority given to such skills in the exam. For example, a perfectly grammatical letter of welcome which sounds unwelcoming in tone would receive lower marks than a letter which is slightly flawed grammatically but which is warm and inviting, on the grounds that the first letter does not communicate effectively. A letter packed with spelling errors would not receive the highest marks even if the grammar was perfect. However, the use of a supplementary grammar book is recommended to support grammar development, particularly for Core candidates. *Recycling Your English* by Clare West (Georgian Press) or *English Grammar in Use* by Raymond Murphy (Cambridge University Press) provide acccessible explanations and exercises. It is important that teachers require students to apply their knowledge of structures after they have been practised, if supplementary books are used.

INTERNATIONAL OVERVIEW

This feature of each unit provides a range of factual and statistical information of global interest and concern, which has been carefully researched from respected sources and is presented via charts, tables and quizzes. It is a device to introduce students to a range of sensitive issues and raise international awareness, and can be delivered in a way the teacher thinks best in his/her particular situation.

The Teacher's notes provide detailed back-up for the Overview and suggestions as to how the information relates to exam topics or previous exam questions. The statistical format can be used to develop the technique of answering exam-type questions on bar charts etc, as set in Papers 1/2, Part 2.

EXAMINER'S TIPS

The Examiner's Tips at the end of each unit fall into two groups: general tips and exam strategy. The first group round off the learning aims and objectives of the unit. They build student independence by developing self-help learning strategies, and allow students to identify individual learning weaknesses and to see what they need to study in more detail or revise. It is important to discuss the general tips fully in class and to ask students to highlight or underline points of special relevance. The tips also contain suggestions for language development outside the class, to further strengthen learner autonomy and responsibility.

The exam strategy tips provide practical guidance about tackling specific exam questions and make a useful reference section. The exam strategies are linked to and consolidate exam exercises introduced and practised in the unit.

UNIT FOCUS

The Unit Focus is an important reference aid enabling students to see a summary of the primary learning aims of the unit, and showing how exercises in the unit cross reference with particular kinds of exam exercises for Core and Extended levels. Students should be encouraged to familiarise themselves with the Unit Focus so as not to be thrown off guard in the exam. For simplicity and clarity, only the main focus of each unit is highlighted, not the wide range of skills that have in fact been covered. It is helpful to get feedback from students about the items in the Unit Focus so that needs for further practice can be diagnosed.

The Unit Focus, in conjunction with the Contents Chart and the 'IGCSE in ESL at a Glance' pages, make a complete reference resource for the teacher, showing how *Success International* develops all the skills required for the IGCSE in ESL.

Managing mixed levels

The following strategies can be used to make certain exercises more accessible for Core candidates aiming for the E-G range. Used with discrimination, they make lessons more stimulating and enjoyable in general.

- The word length given in the exam-format writing questions can be lowered by 50 words, making it equivalent to the Core requirements.

- Simpler words such as *come* can be added to the spelling lists, or used to replace some of the more difficult words on the spelling lists.

- Whole-class teaching can deliver information about a topic before students take part in a problem-solving exercise.

- Small tests can be given at the start of each lesson to check that key points in the previous lesson have been assimilated.

- If a largely Core group is going to listen to an Extended-type listening text, some of the gaps in gapped notes can be filled in by the teacher beforehand. If the question format is short answer, which Core candidates are not set, the short answer questions could be answered orally, not in writing.

- An exercise can simply be divided in half and allocated to two groups in the class so there is less for each group to do.

- Students can be encouraged to learn a few selected items on a list of phrasal verbs etc, rather than trying to learn the complete list.

- The 'jigsaw technique' can be used to break a whole task down into component parts. The class is put into groups and groups are assigned their components to complete, with weaker groups being given easier tasks. New groups are then formed, consisting of one representative from each of the old groups. Each representative is responsible for reporting the answers for his/her component part of the task. In the end, all the students have a complete set of answers.

Happiness and Success

OVERVIEW

The main aims of this unit are: to develop an orientation to study, including spelling strategies, choosing a dictionary and keeping work organised; to develop more sophisticated comprehension skills; to develop a more mature style for describing people, both friends/close relatives and people admired from a distance.

THEME

The theme of this unit is happiness, an intriguing topic which should provoke plenty of discussion. The main areas for discussion are

(a) personal:

- What makes you happy?

- If you are feeling unhappy, what kind of things can you do about it?

- Would setting goals give you more control of your life or make you feel more pressurised?

(b) more abstract:

- Should the right to happiness be placed above other considerations?

- What are the principles of a happy life?

- Do achievement and success bring happiness, or does happiness come from inside you, out of the person you are?

The reading items are a quiz on happiness from a popular magazine, a chatty magazine article about one woman's way of being happy, an interview with someone whose happiness comes from having overcome a major drawback – illiteracy, and comments about David Bellamy, the international environmentalist. A sense of self-worth is essential for a happy outlook, and all the 'characters' reveal it in some way or other.

Students also listen to a radio interviewer asking a journalist whether the sacrifice of personal happiness is indeed the 'price of greatness'.

LANGUAGE WORK

Students' vocabulary is enlarged through work on homophones, figurative language, adjectival collocations and colour imagery.

Spelling (a complex area) is demystified through consideration of the links between speech sounds and spelling patterns, spelling rules and silent letters. The 'look, say, cover, write, check' method is introduced as an all-round approach to learning new spellings quickly.

Reading comprehension is extended through work on deductive reasoning skills, an area in which IGCSE candidates consistently underperform.

The exam requires that students describe people in a way that digs below the surface to reveal personality and character. They also need to produce reasoned descriptions. Students learn to do this by analysing how a mature descriptive style is attained: using more complex clauses and a wider vocabulary, and by evidence to support opinions.

What is happiness?

1 Quiz

As this is the first lesson in the course, you may like to use a little time before you start the unit to answer students' main queries about the IGCSE in ESL exam, what it involves and how the course will help them achieve the exam requirements. Let them know that the end of each unit has a section of exam-format questions, followed by examiner's tips and a summary of the main areas focused on in the unit.

The topic of happiness is introduced through a quiz. Quizzes are fascinating and fun to do, and students will soon feel drawn into completing the quiz. Tell them not to worry about each individual word but to try to understand the gist of the language. The scores are on page 191 of their book.

2 Discussion

A The quiz suggests that people who are living their life by a set of clear personal values are the happiest. However, this is a culturally loaded notion and you might like to ask:

'Is self-sacrifice necessary for the benefit of family or community?'
'Is it right to put your own happiness before anything else? Where would you draw the line?'

B & C Now let the discussion become more personal. Encourage students to discuss the little things which make them feel happy. You could suggest some specific things which make you feel happy as examples first.

To help them focus their reasoning and expressive powers, ask them to give specific examples. This clarifies their thinking from the general to the particular. You could suggest, for instance, that instead of saying *'I feel happy when I see friends'* they say *'I feel happy when I go swimming with my closest friends from school.'*

D It's also interesting to explore what students can do if they *don't* feel happy. You could start by asking them to identify specific causes of unhappiness, e.g. being refused permission to stay out late, not being chosen for the school team. You could ask *'What can help you feel better?'* Answers might be: talking to a close friend about how he/she coped in a similar situation or deciding to do your best to forget about it by doing something enjoyable and comforting, such as absorbing yourself in a favourite hobby or interest.

You could extend the exercise if students are interested enough by categorising strategies for overcoming unhappy feelings into two types: things which require the support or help of other people, and things which you can do alone to help yourself. The latter could include: writing in a journal or diary, writing to a friend, finding quiet time to reflect.

3 Formal and informal styles

Students will be developing their awareness of formal and informal styles throughout the course. It will be interesting to ask them when they think it is appropriate to use the different styles (informal for friends, school newsletters and family; more formal for newspapers and factual writing). It's also worth reminding them that the styles are not totally rigid. Serious writing will use occasional colloquialisms and idiomatic expressions.

ANSWERS

1B **2**E **3**A **4**C **5**D

4 Spelling patterns and speech sounds

The exam is looking for the ability to spell reasonably well. Students are expected to be able to spell high-frequency words without difficulty, e.g. *book, magazine, people*. If the exam reading comprehension questions require answers containing words which are difficult to spell, the actual words can usually be found in the text itself. Students should be told to copy out carefully the correct spellings from the text. However, English spelling is a hugely complex area and the exam recognises this. The occasional spelling mistake,

therefore, is not disastrous and will not prevent a highly able student receiving an A grade.

The letter *q* in English is always followed by the letter *u*. The sound is usually /kw/ but you may like to elicit some exceptions, e.g. *cheque, quay, quiche, queue*, after the students have completed the exercise.

ANSWERS

1 queen
2 quotation
3 quack
4 banquet

Elicit examples of other speech sounds and spelling patterns.

Examples:
ck at the end of words, pronounced /k/: *lock, tick, sock*
ch pronounced /tʃ/: *church, patch, change*
ch pronounced /k/: *chemist, technology, mechanic*
sh pronounced /ʃ/: *shout, push, mushroom*

5 Approaches to spelling

The aim here is to draw out students' previous knowledge of spelling patterns and to make them more conscious. After they have ticked the strategies they use to help them spell, you could ask them what they do about words they always misspell.

6 Look, say, cover, write, check

This is an uncomplicated method of memorising spellings by strengthening visual recall. There is a similar exercise in every unit. Students who have not encountered the method may be resistant to it because they feel daunted by the thought of learning every new spelling individually. It's a good idea to emphasise the simplicity of the method. When they get the hang of it, students can learn spellings fast, effectively and with a lower failure rate than with many other methods. Of course, they'll also be using other methods, such as spelling rules and how speech sounds are linked to spelling patterns.

7 Tricky words

These tricky words are often spelled wrongly by IGCSE candidates. Ask students to say each word aloud clearly to check pronunciation. It's useful to ask for a definition or example sentence for each word.

Students should go through the 'look, say, cover, write, check' method to memorise the spelling of each tricky word. It's important they don't miss out any steps. Once they feel confident that they have imprinted the image of the word on their mind, they should write it three times.

8 Why are words misspelled?

The aim of this exercise is to activate students' understanding of why spelling mistakes are made. This is a vast subject area and the exercise highlights a few of the most common problems as a starting point. You can start by asking *Which words do you always misspell?* Students are often aware of their own weak points, such as confusing the endings of words which have similar sounds but a different spelling.

Encourage them to work together to brainstorm all their ideas. Tell them to concentrate on exploring ideas about words rather than being 'right'. The resulting discussion will probably be heated and perhaps even chaotic. It doesn't really matter, however, as students should see this a trial-and-error process. There'll be plenty of time in ensuing lessons to remedy any misconceptions about silent letters, etc. Encourage them to think about the root of the problem.

When 'ps' or 'pn' begin a word, the 'p' is silent. Other examples: *psalm, pseudonym, pneumonia*.

Words like *truthful* are often spelled wrongly because the addition of the suffix to *truth* sounds like '*full*'. Other examples: *peaceful, hopeful, playful*.

Activities is sometimes misspelled because students forget the rule that a 'y' ending changes to 'ies' if the preceding letter is a consonant. Other examples: *ceremonies, lorries, factories, families, babies, ladies*. Words with a vowel before the final 'y' simply add 's' to make a plural: *boys, holidays, highways*.

The ending of *responsible* is often misspelled '*able*'. Other adjectives ending in *-ible* are *edible, incredible, invisible*. But many words end in *-able*, e.g. *washable, reliable, advisable, excitable, approachable*. There is no simple rule for choosing the right ending. Tell students it's better to learn each spelling through the 'look, say, cover, write, check' method.

Calm has a silent 'l'. Other examples: *talk, yolk, almond*.

Committee probably presents problems because students are not sure whether to use a single or double 'm' and 't'.

Honour is often misspelled because of the silent 'h'. Other examples are: *hour, humour, exhibition, exhaust*. Sometimes the 'u' in *honour/colour* is left out due to the influence of American spelling.

Curable presents similar problems to *responsible*.

Embarrassment presents similar difficulties to *committee*, as does *accommodation*. Each of these words has *two* sets of double consonants.

Wrist has a silent 'w'. Other examples of a silent 'w': *write, wrap, wrinkle, wrestle*.

Students' spelling errors don't always fall into neat categories. Some errors are just idiosyncratic. Encourage students to proof-read their work for careless spelling errors, paying particular attention to words that present difficulties for them as individuals. Remind them that learning to spell is a lifelong process. However highly educated you are, there will always be a need to memorise the spelling of a new word, ask how to spell a person's name etc, or look a word up in a dictionary.

9 How helpful is your dictionary?

Somehow students feel reassured by dictionaries, especially 'weighty' volumes. They feel the mere sight of them guarantees success! Others prefer modern electronic dictionaries.

Make sure students understand that the dictionary they choose must make sense to them. It is simply a tool, of no use unless it can work for them. It should be neither too complex nor too low-level. If you have a mixed ability class (and who doesn't?), you may find there is no perfect dictionary suitable for the range. You may like to bring in a variety of dictionaries, or get students to pool and compare their own dictionaries, using the brief checklist as a guide.

It might be helpful to do some follow-up work on the abbreviations used in dictionaries, and the extra features some dictionaries have. These might include a key to pronunciation, tables of weights and measures, or explanations of common acronyms.

Dictionaries are such wonderful sources of information, it's good to make them a regular feature of language learning. You can integrate dictionary work with other projects and in other curriculum areas. Students sometimes respond best to dictionary work which is linked to practical applications (as part of a reading comprehension or during a writing task, for example) rather than work on a dictionary for its own sake.

10 Getting organised

When students start a new course of study, they need to be well organised. However, being organised just does not come easily to many of us. It's a good idea to remind students it is something to work at and take responsibility for. It's very frustrating for everybody if a class member cannot find his/her notes from the last lesson which are to serve as an outline plan for an essay etc. Remind students that the work in the course is sequential and they need to keep lesson notes carefully, as they will need them later. Showing how a file can be organised, with dividers etc, perhaps using a well kept file as an example, can be very helpful.

Some teachers like to set a special, regular time for organisation of course notes and spelling/vocabulary books.

Happy not to be a high flyer

11 Before you read

A Eliciting students' responses to the photograph is a good way to introduce the topic of describing people. Tina has a particularly bright smile. You might like to elicit other collocations for smile, e.g. *a shy smile, a tender smile, a half-smile, a friendly smile, a warm smile, a dazzling smile.*

You could ask students to study Tina's eyes for clues to her character, e.g. *'Does she look confident/cold/ secretive/guarded/shy/warm/ nervous?'*

B The text comes from a women's magazine. It is lighthearted and chatty and gives a practical illustration of someone who has a calm and happy outlook.

VOCABULARY CHECK: ANSWERS

a priority: something you think is more important than other things
insignificant: of little importance
trivial: similar in meaning to insignificant

12 Comprehension check

ANSWERS

1 They feel she could achieve more/she is only an assistant.
2 Her family
3 Because she realises more responsibility at work would involve too many personal sacrifices.
4 Her attitude to life is positive. She makes the most of the life she has.

13 Principles of a happy life

Students should have fun working out the 'dos and don'ts' of these 'principles', which are based on modern counselling approaches. They may disagree about some, and it will be interesting to explore why. You could discuss, for instance, the problem of over-generalising. You could ask:

'Is it really a bad idea to try to impress other people?'
'Is it always harmful to regret decisions you made in the past?'

14 Finding examples

IGCSE students find matching abstract ideas to concrete examples hard because it involves thinking about how theories can be applied in practice. They may find their ideas difficult to express accurately, but this is not a big problem as the exercise is focusing on developing understanding rather than extending technical ability. Ask them to concentrate on getting their message across in the group, rather than grammatical accuracy. After the groups have thought through their ideas, you may like to elicit the main points and write them up for everybody.

POSSIBLE ANSWERS

She says her mother wanted her to have a job with more status but this hasn't troubled her. This shows she doesn't hold resentment against her parents.

She says her relationships are more important to her than academic or career success, which shows she doesn't value status or material things more than people.

She says she realises how tied down she is when friends go off travelling, but she accepts that she cannot do this. This shows she doesn't envy other people.

She says she doesn't want a more senior role at work because that would mean another part of her life would suffer. This shows she is realistic about what she can achieve.

The pleasure of her job comes from feeling it's worthwhile rather than the status of it, which shows she has chosen a job which gives her real satisfaction.

15 Sharing ideas

The concept of 'happiness principles' will vary according to the interests and maturity of your group. Extra ideas to discuss could be:

Don't let small worries take over your life.
Do try to take responsibility for solving your problems.
Do give the important people in your life most of your attention.
Don't spend time with people who make you miserable.
Do try to be peaceful.

16 Discussion

You could introduce the discussion topic by asking students:

'How far is it worth giving up daily pleasures in order to have success later?'
'Can you have everything? Is part of maturity accepting that you can't?'

17 Goal setting

In this exercise, students explore the value of setting goals. Setting goals helps to give a sense of control and direction in life. It may be a strange idea to some students who have thought no further than 'My ideal career'! You can focus the exercise by giving further examples of immediate goals (telephone a friend, return library books), medium-term goals (complete school project, save up for new clothes) and long-term goals (train as a pilot, have a house of my own).

The exercise could open into an interesting discussion about when you should change your goals. You could ask: *'What would you say to someone whose goal was to become a ballet dancer/athlete? At 14 he/she is told he/she's too tall/the wrong build to ever be successful.'*

18 Figurative meanings

The English language is packed with figurative expressions and idioms. You could introduce the exercise by adapting a phrase from the reading passage: '*When Tina's friends travel abroad, she feels tied down.*' You could ask '*Is she tied down by ropes or is it just a feeling?*'

ANSWERS

1 wrestling
2 lifts
3 squashed
4 fighting
5 broke
6 battling
7 buried
8 crippled

Some other common expressions are:

a broken heart, a polished performance, a shining example, a glowing reference, an explosive argument, a stormy relationship.

It would be very interesting to elicit examples of figurative expressions in the students' own language(s).

19 Homophones

Check your students' pronunciation of the homophones as it is important that they produce sounds which are exactly the same. Sometimes students confuse minimal pairs, e.g. *still/steal, live/leave*, with homophones.

ANSWERS

1 place
2 pain
3 peace
4 whole
5 allowed
6 pear
7 sight
8 There
9 four
10 sore

20 More homophones

ANSWERS

1 steel
2 mail
3 you're
4 weak
5 our
6 bare
7 tale
8 sail
9 pour/pore
10 whale

The English language has a relatively wide variety of homophones. Again it would be interesting to elicit examples from your students' own language(s).

The price of greatness

21 Before you listen

The listening is an interview about the theories in a book 'The Price of Greatness'. The speaker suggests that a disproportionate number of great, original thinkers have suffered from ill health or genetic disability, or come from lonely, stressful backgrounds. The speaker ends by suggesting that ordinary children can do very well through hard work, without undue sacrifices or mental strain.

The pre-listening exercise is important as it gets students thinking about someone they admire and exploring reasons for their views. Remind them, as always, to keep their notes as they will need them later.

(The photographs are of Mahatma Gandhi and Princess Diana.)

22 Vocabulary check

ANSWERS

1G 2F 3B 4A 5C 6D 7E

23 Listening: Radio interview

The comprehension questions focus on the attitudes of the speaker and the interviewer. This is an area which is very challenging for IGCSE students as it requires a sophisticated appreciation of the nuances of language.

Let students hear the whole conversation through once to get the gist. After they have listened, you could ask some basic comprehension questions such as '*Does Steve think great thinkers had happy lives? Why/Why not?*'

Let them listen a second or third time, pausing the tape if necessary. When you check the comprehension, replay any parts of the conversation over which there is confusion or disagreement.

ANSWERS

1b 2a 3c 4b

TAPESCRIPT

Listen to this radio interview and choose the best answer for each question.

INTERVIEWER: And time now for our interview of the day and my guest in the studio this afternoon is Steve Bowman. Steve's been reading an absolutely wonderful book, so he tells me, all about how you may have to sacrifice a lot of personal happiness if you genuinely want to achieve great things. Steve, what's the book called and can you please tell us what makes great achievers different from everyone else?

STEVE: Well, the main thing as I understand in this book, *The Price of Greatness* by Professor Ludwig, which is truly a fascinating study of great and original thinkers, Einstein, Picasso and so on, is that they have an enormous ... an enormous inner drive to succeed.

I: Hmmm. Far higher, you'd say, than the average person?

S: Much higher. And then there's the inborn talent. It's suggested in the book that you need a precise blend of brain chemicals which are inherited.

I: So parents do play a part?

S: Yes, indeed. But what is a lot more surprising is how much ... how much the environment plays in extraordinary achievement. Most people aren't aware of the setbacks these people suffered. Did you realise that a huge number of gifted people lost a parent before the age of 14? Others suffered from, you know ... a genetic disability of some kind. Or had a major illness like polio or TB before adulthood.

I: So Steinbeck wouldn't have become a great writer if he hadn't had pneumonia as a teenager?

S: That sort of idea, yes.

I: Ah, well, I ... I don't know. Surely a great many people got terrible illnesses, they lost a mum or dad – well especially if you're talking about the past – and they didn't go on to split the atom (or) whatever.

S: It's the combination of many factors that's important. Obviously, many people have got ... got problems but are not going to be the next Nobel prizewinner. With great achievers, you can't just pick out one or two factors. It's a very complex web.

I: What other factors might you reasonably expect to find?

S: Clever but frustrated parents, erm, possibly brothers and sisters who they may have close but difficult relationships with, all these factors ...

I: But you would expect these ... well, these setbacks to be, er, very damaging to their future chances, wouldn't you? And you're saying they were not, in fact?

S: It seems that such children suffered from a feeling of ... well, a ... a feeling of inferiority, of not being good enough, which pushed them onwards to achieve more and more.

I: Hmmm. So as adults, many of them will have ended with a very unhappy emotional life though, won't they?

S: They've probably suffered from depression ... what Professor Ludwig calls a sense of psychological unease.

I: Well, Steve, you've told us about the very many drawbacks these people have. What does the budding genius seem to need?

S: Peace and quiet. They need to bury themselves in work. As children, they're loners and spend a lot of time by themselves.

I: And what might you tell parents who might ... well, you know ... might like to think they're bringing up the next Nobel prizewinner?

S: If you want your child to be well, you know, well adjusted, forget about greatness. If you want your child to be kind to others and what have you, you're cutting down your child's chances to excel.

I: Do any of us want children growing up burdened with ... well you've described it very well as psychological unease?

S: Yes, it ... it may be that the ... the sacrifice of personal happiness may indeed be the price of greatness. But, er, I wouldn't say that you ought to stop trying to achieve your potential.   Er ... think of it this way: you might have an ordinary kid, who, well, mightn't be the next superstar, the next Picasso, but everyone's got their own ... their own individual potential. You've got to make the most of that.

I: So how can ordinary children fulfil themselves?

S: Studies have shown that ordinary children who are well balanced in their lives but achieve a lot – they play football for school leagues, or win prizes for chess, art, music or whatever – well, it's 5% talent and the rest is hard work.

I: Ah ha! So you're saying you don't have to give up all enjoyment – it's important to keep a balance, isn't it?

S: That's right. You can still have time to do the things you want to do.

I: Thank you, Steve. It's good to end on that positive note.

24 Post-listening discussion

A Students could relate the question of (un)happiness and creativity to examples of well-known achievers in their own culture(s).

B It will be very interesting to hear students' responses to the idea that ordinary children can reach a high standard of achievement mostly through hard work. It would be interesting to explore how far other factors, apart from talent, can help achievement, e.g. a good teacher, financial support, parental encouragement.

25 Apostrophes (1)

This exercise is to be done deductively, as students will probably have some prior familiarity with the use of apostrophes. Encourage them to pool their ideas to work out why they are used here (to show the omission of letters).

You could extend the exercise by writing on the board a few examples of sentences without contractions and asking them where the apostrophes would go if contractions were used, e.g. *He might have told us he would be late.* *They were not happy with the results.*

PRONUNCIATION

Even when students are able to hear contractions, they frequently have difficulty incorporating them into their own speech. Remind them that, although using a non-contracted form (e.g. *She would not come*) conveys meaning accurately, it sounds stilted and much less fluent than the use of a contracted form.

26 Apostrophes (2)

The aim of this exercise is to reflect the main problems IGCSE students have with the apostrophe. These are:

a) using it whenever there is a plural, whether or not possession is signified;
b) failing to put the apostrophe where the missing letter or letters would be in a contraction;
c) confusing the position of the apostrophe when it is used to show possession. Remind students that if the noun is singular, *'s* is added: *my mother's garden.* If the noun is plural ending in 's', an apostrophe is added *after* the 's': *my parents' house.* But students are often confused by plural nouns which do *not* end in 's'; these need *'s: the people's leader, a children's home.*

You could extend the exercise by writing up a few phrases which show possession without apostrophes, e.g.

a field belonging to a farmer
a dining room for students
a library for children
a dress belonging to Mary.

Then ask students to substitute phrases which use apostrophes, e.g. *a students' dining room.*

27 Correcting sentences

ANSWERS

1   The teachers listened to Carol's views.
2   They've bought a new car.
3   I went to my mother's office.
4   Please don't touch the babies' clothes.
5   It's hard to explain the programme's success.
6   She works in the women's ward of the hospital.
7   He's training to be a ladies' hairdresser.
8   You'll find her in the teachers' workroom – all the staff go there.
9   He might've become the next Einstein.
10   She couldn't understand why her cat had lost its appetite.

Monitor students' pronunciation of these sentences.

28 Speculating about a photograph

The aim of this exercise is to develop students' ability to describe people. They study a photograph of David Bellamy (who they probably will not recognise) and read the comments describing him. The exam is looking for the ability to provide more than a physical description. Students need to describe character and give reasons for their opinions, so this is a good opportunity to widen their vocabulary and help them frame opinions.

You can prompt them where necessary, e.g. *'Does he look as if he has suffered/had a hard life?, Does he look disappointed/discontented?, Does he look as if he could cope in a crisis? Why/Why not?'*

Write up on the board any interesting adjectives students suggest, e.g. *cheerful, weathered, mellow, wise.*

You might like to give students more information about David Bellamy. He grew up in the English countryside, in an ordinary working-class family. The family had almost no books until his father bought a set of encyclopedias. David learned a great deal about the wider world by reading these. He also explored the countryside around his home and he noticed how nature had the power to adapt and restore itself. He is now a writer, environmental consultant and campaigner. He has led protests about the destruction of the rainforests and has campaigned for the protection of the environment on a world-wide scale.

29 Describing personal qualities

This exercise will help to develop students' powers of deductive reasoning. It builds on the skills they developed earlier, in exercise 14, where they looked for practical examples of 'happiness principles'.

ANSWERS

1 yes **2** yes **3** no **4** yes **5** yes **6** no **7** yes **8** yes **9** yes **10** no

You could discuss why answers are right or wrong and get students to supply evidence from the anecdotes.

One of David's key ideas is the belief that nature can restore itself. It would be interesting to develop this concept further by analogy with the body. For example, you could ask *'When is the body self-healing? Do you always need medicine for an illness?'*

30 Discussion

Now that students have read the comments about David, you may like to ask them to look again at his photo and see if the qualities described are visible in his face. You could ask, for example, *'Is his strength of mind revealed in his face?'*

The discussion could be extended to think about the qualities necessary for achievement. It would be nice for students to consider whether their particular heroes/heroines have these qualities. You could ask them for practical examples of the way the qualities are expressed.

31 Drafting a paragraph

Students should write a paragraph describing David. They can mention his appearance and, more importantly, describe his qualities. They should give examples of his views as a way of illustrating his qualities.

POSSIBLE ANSWER

A possible paragraph could run something like this:

David looks warm and easy-going but he is very determined and hard-working. He has great optimism and belief in the powers of nature to adapt. In spite of our environmental problems, he is positive about the possibility of improvement. He believes in himself and can tolerate criticism. For instance, his view that the countryside should be managed is unpopular with many people. He is prepared to suffer for his beliefs, and even went to prison in a battle to save the rainforests.

Encourage students to discuss their first draft with a partner. Remind them that rewriting is not a sign of failure, but simply part of the writing process.

Obstacles and challenges

32 Expressing fears and giving reassurance

Students study and practise the functional language in pairs. You could elicit from them the things they find nerve-wracking and incorporate them into the practice.

You might like to elicit other phrases students may know to express fear, e.g. *I really dread ..., I panic when I think about it*.

PRACTICE

Students can practise expressing fears and giving reassurance in pairs. You could ask a pair of students who have done particularly well to perform an example to the whole class.

33 Pre-reading discussion

Students are going to read an article about a woman who was illiterate. She explains how her unhappy school days resulted in not learning to read. She disguised her problem, not even telling her husband, until the headteacher at her daughter's school asked her to take a job as a paid helper. The headteacher had recognised Monica's illiteracy and helped her to learn to read. Now Monica works as a 'parent educator'; she involves parents in the education of their children.

34 Vocabulary check

ANSWERS

taunted: made fun of
illiterate: unable to read or write
volunteer: person who works without pay, often for a charity etc.

35 Reading: Textual organisation

Before students start reading, you could ask them to predict something about the content of the article from the title.

ANSWERS

A7 **B**2 **C**1 **D**5 **E**3 **F**6 **G**4

36 Comprehension check

It's important for students to realise that adult illiteracy in England is unusual (although more common than is realised), in order for them to empathize with the embarrassment Monica felt. It also explains why Monica would feel she could not 'join in the life other people were living'.

ANSWERS

1   She disliked school because she had an intimidating class teacher/the other children made fun of her/she did not understand the lessons.

2   Maggie hid the fact she couldn't read by saying she'd left her glasses at home, or she'd carry a book or newspaper around and pretend to read it.
3   She was terrified.
4   She has learned that she has to make the most of her opportunities.

37 Vocabulary: Odd one out

ANSWERS

1   robust
2   abrasive
3   timid

38 'Bird' idioms

The expression '*she took me under her wing*' means she looked after and guided Monica when she had no obligation to do so.

ANSWERS

1   an ugly duckling
2   a bird's eye view
3   a hen party
4   a bird in the hand is worth two in the bush
5   took her under her wing
6   kill two birds with one stone

39 Post-reading discussion

It will be interesting to hear students' views in this discussion. It's common for young people (like many of us) to think they would be happier if their lives were easier, if they had more material things or a different family. It's rewarding to help them become more realistic and to encourage them to consider how they might have to mature and adapt to real life to get more fulfilment.

Maggie took responsibility for changing herself from an insecure, illiterate woman to the person she is today. Her happiness seems to come from having satisfying work, being able to join in with ordinary life and from her daughter's success. Her 'achievements' are linked to her personal qualities. She is able to persevere to reach a goal, to be honest about herself, to give to others and to show warmth. In this sense her happiness has come out of the person she is.

An interesting theme to draw out in discussion is 'How can someone with a low self-image gain self-esteem?' You could link the responses to the example set by Monica.

INTERNATIONAL OVERVIEW

The acronym UNICEF stands for United Nations (International) Children's (Emergency) Fund.

An interesting question arising from the facts given for the class to ponder could be: '*Why are more women than men illiterate?*' This could lead to a lively discussion about social customs.

In many countries, girls are expected to devote a lot of time to very basic household and family duties, e.g. fetching water and fuel to cook with, thus robbing them of time to go to school. Also in some countries schooling is very expensive and the opportunity is given to the male members of the household. As always, encourage students to relate the information to the situation in their own countries. You could point out that in many of the world's affluent nations, it was the custom to give priority to boys' education until relatively recently.

40 Describing people

Striking tells us that Sally is unusually attractive.

One, two or three well-chosen adjectives before a noun have a stronger effect than several over-familiar ones.

The description of Sally's smile emphasises her spontaneity, her openness and her warmth. Her relationship with her mother seems exceptionally close. The writer achieves this effect by using the word '*overflowing*', which suggests an abundance, with no limit to the love Sally feels.

41 Using a wide range of adjectives

The aim of this exercise is to look at a variety of ways of describing people. These include using fresher adjectives and compounds. Students should focus on both appearance and character because they are expected to show awareness of both in the exam. Elicit other examples of adjectives and adjective compounds.

42 Adjective collocations / 43 Positive and negative

Instead of working in pairs, students could be divided into four groups and each group assigned to one of the headings.

ANSWERS

APPEARANCE
slim ✓, well-proportioned ✓, plump, balding ✗, burly, rugged, well-dressed ✓, rangy, elegant ✓, scruffy ✗, overweight ✗, skinny ✗

HAIR
wavy, straight, wispy ✗, (balding ✗), luxuriant ✓, curly-haired, close-cropped, bushy

VOICE
deep, grating ✗, husky, melodious ✓, quiet, high-pitched, gentle ✓

CHARACTER
tight-fisted ✗, genial ✓, shy, placid, ambitious, tolerant ✓, absent-minded, tender-hearted ✓, quiet, self-centred ✗, dreamy, ill-mannered ✗, altruistic ✓, generous ✓, considerate ✓, outgoing ✓, gentle ✓, argumentative ✗, bad-tempered ✗, domineering ✗, frank, humorous ✓

Point out that the connotation of some words is subjective, e.g. *ambitious* will sound positive to some people and negative to others.

44 Negative prefixes

It's useful to compare the way opposites are formed in English with students' own language(s).

ANSWERS

irresponsible
insecure
unreliable
unhappy
discontented
immature
untrustworthy
inefficient
disloyal
dishonest

45 Colour

Focusing on the role of colour in appearance will help make students' writing more vivid. You could ask them to liken each other's colouring and clothes to images in the natural world.

BEING CREATIVE

Students could read their sentences aloud to each other for fun and feedback.

46 Developing a more mature style

Students hoping for the highest marks in the exam will need to show a degree of linguistic sophistication. The following sequence of exercises builds on the earlier work on adjectives and collocations, etc. The exercises will help students structure more complex sentences and bring variety into their styles of writing.

Make sure students understand the meaning of the individual words in each quotation when they underline the clauses.

47 Conveying character traits

This exercise helps students understand how writers achieve their effects – in this case, by the psychological associations of the words chosen. Let them know that the extract describes an adult, not a child, before they begin to study it.

Analysing how a writer achieves his/her effects is very challenging. You will probably want to monitor students' analysis quite closely, prompt them with questions where necessary and give feedback on their work.

For example, through the description '*She was a tall, fragile-looking woman in a pretty blue hat that matched her eyes*' the writer conveys the impression that the woman is feminine and ladylike. To help students understand this, you could ask '*Do you think she would be the type of woman who would be a tough businesswoman? Why/Why not?*'

You could ask '*What does the fact that she is wearing a pretty blue hat that matched her eyes suggest about her?*', eliciting that she is carefully dressed, perhaps in a slightly old-fashioned or traditional way. She is not taking risks with her appearance! The choice of the word *pretty* suggests that the hat is attractive but not too bold or daring. '*Is blue an exciting or a quiet, soothing colour? What does that tell us about her?*'

You could ask '*What does fragile-looking suggest about her?*', eliciting that she doesn't look particularly strong or robust. She looks delicate, gentle and ladylike.

48 Writing your own description

Students will need enough time to write up a description of a friend if they are to do it justice. Remind them before they start that integrating what they have learned earlier about using clauses, descriptive phrases, etc will make their writing much stronger.

FEEDBACK

Encourage positive but specific criticism so that students really benefit. For example, '*I liked the way you showed that he is a methodical person by explaining that he keeps all his CDs and books neatly, and in alphabetical order.*'

Someone I admire

49 Model description

Students should study the model description, which reflects earlier themes of self-acceptance and developing inner strength. It displays elements of the linguistic sophistication the exam is encouraging them to develop. The standard is purposely high so that even 'A' students in your class have something to work towards.

As always in the coursebook, the model writing shows a range of things students could say, and aims to stimulate creativity. Although based on exam-type questions, models are *not* meant to be learned by heart to be reproduced in the exam.

The main topic of each paragraph is:

1 Simon's appearance and character traits
2 Why the writer admires Simon
3 Why Simon is a good friend
4 Conclusion

COMPREHENSION CHECK: SUGGESTED ANSWERS

1 He gives the impression of being studious, particular in his habits, and not concerned about his appearance.
2 He was unhappy at school because the other students taunted him and called him 'ugly duckling'.

3 Simon is determined because he was painfully shy but he overcame this through his own efforts.
4 The writer values Simon's friendship because he is trustworthy and straightforward and helped him face his fears.

FORMAT

This exercise helps students to see how all the techniques are used in combination.

50 Comparing two styles

The aim of this exercise is to show students how a more mature style can be achieved. It also shows the value of drafting work and taking advice. Encourage your students to see that the style of the first draft could be improved by the use of clauses and more vivid description.

51 Rewriting with more sophistication

Students could produce something like this:

My friend has large, sparkling green eyes and close-cropped blonde hair. She smiles often, showing her lovely white teeth. She is well-dressed with a style of her own. She enjoys studying other people and says she can judge their character from their clothes. She is a very hard-working student who gets high marks. She is kind, considerate and generous and never minds helping me with my homework.

52 Writing from notes

Many students will have heard of Lister and the theory of antisepsis from science classes. Lister was influenced by Pasteur's germ theory, which claimed that bacteria can cause disease, and that fermentation and rotting are caused by bacteria which live in the air. It would be nice to let students outline the main ideas before they tackle the rewriting from notes.

This is a good time to remind students that they can sometimes draw on knowledge from other areas of the curriculum to answer exam questions. However, they will have to make their knowledge fit properly into the context of the question. It would also be interesting here to ask about notable scientific advances made by scientists from the students' own culture(s).

It's worth highlighting '*anti*' as a prefix meaning 'to counteract or be opposite to'. Other examples to elicit could be: *antidote, antibody, antibiotic, anticlockwise, antiperspirant, antisocial.*

MODEL ANSWER

I want to describe Joseph Lister. He was a surgeon who was born in 1827. In those days many patients died after operations because their wounds became badly infected. Lister wondered if (the) bacteria in the air which made meat decay also made wounds septic.

Lister decided to clean everything which touched (the) patients' wounds with carbolic acid. The carbolic acid destroyed all the germs/Carbolic acid destroys all germs. As a result of these precautions, patients recovered quickly after/from (their) operations. The rate of infection fell dramatically.

Lister developed safe, antiseptic operations, which was a major medical advance. He received many awards for his work. I admire him because he was dedicated and unselfish. He took great personal risks to make this discovery. Surgery used to be highly dangerous. People were terrified of the surgeon's knife. Lister changed all that. Modern surgery is a life-saver.

WIDER PRACTICE

1   Students could further develop their skills for describing clothing. Mail-order clothes catalogues and magazines are a rich source of pictures to stimulate descriptive writing. Students may enjoy, for example, looking through clothes catalogues and choosing outfits for each other. They could write descriptions of the outfits using clothes vocabulary. It's good to elicit relevant vocabulary, e.g. *short-sleeved, with a zip, lace-trimmed, made of leather*, before this exercise.

2   Tell students to imagine that they have the chance to refurbish a common room or classroom. They are to choose the colours, the fabrics and the furnishings. Encourage them to study the paint charts and fabric catalogues manufacturers produce (which have an astonishing variety of ways of describing shades of colour, patterns, etc) if they are available where you teach. They could write up the article for the school newsletter.

3   Magazines, and TV and radio programmes often run interviews with well-known people in which they describe key stages in their personal development. This can make an interesting follow-up to the work on happiness and life's challenges, especially if it is a personality students can identify with.

Students could be set this work as a project to research in their own language and present a translation to the class, if English-speaking TV etc is not easily available.

4   To help students develop their ability to link character with appearance, you could bring into the class some particularly powerful or emotive photographs of people cut from magazines, etc. Alternatively, you could freeze a video frame of a striking character on a videotape.

You could then ask students to study all the details of the person's appearance: facial expression, body language, clothing, shoes, accessories, hairstyle, etc. You could ask questions like:

What kind of person is he/she? What clues do we have from his/her appearance?
What is he/she thinking?
What do you think his/her home life is like?
What kind of job do you think he/she does?
What are his/her values and outlook on things?

Encourage students to be as speculative as possible, as there are no right answers. Students could follow up this exercise with some creative writing in which they build a situation around the character.

You and Your Community

OVERVIEW

The main aim of this unit is to develop the skills students need to give information about self, family and home locality. In the exam, home background and personal interests are contextualised within a community context. The unit culminates in writing a letter of welcome to an overseas exchange visitor.

THEME AND SKILLS

The theme of the unit is home and community life. In addition to personal description in this area of the exam, students are required to comment on local community issues etc in the role of responsible citizen. Through discussion, reading, listening and role play the following issues are raised:

- how best to impart information about ourselves and our life orally
- how we come to form impressions of individuals and their background
- how we can describe a favourite place in our locality in a way which makes our listeners enthusiastic too
- how to present ourselves positively in writing
- in our role as citizens, how we engage with the needs of our community.

Students study a newspaper feature called 'Home Town' and a magazine article on fostering children. They listen to a discussion about whether to convert a disused warehouse into a study centre or a youth club.

LANGUAGE WORK

The challenge this aspect of the exam presents for students is being able to put themselves across appropriately. They need to be able to go beyond factual description and provide the revealing glimpses about their lives which create a vivid picture of who they are. This requires not only being able to choose from a wide vocabulary, but also demands an understanding of how impressions are created, and the language resources to shape the impression they wish to make. The unit tackles these difficulties by providing analysis and practice in presenting themselves orally and in writing, by developing their reading strategies and by giving attention to the functions of language and register.

Students' understanding of spelling is enlarged through studying the rules for doubling the consonant in one- and two-syllable words. Vocabulary development focuses on words for describing places and people, loan words from other languages, and colloquial language in context.

Home town

1 Interview / 2 Group A / 3 Group B

The aim of this role-play interview is to set students talking freely and openly about their home life. Setting up an in-depth interview in the classroom is more difficult than it often appears. A common problem is lack of interviewing skills. This exercise is based on an exam-style exercise in which, of course, the interviewer would be the examiner. You may like to consider ways of maximising the potential of the interview, perhaps by choosing your most able students to act as interviewer or by 'borrowing' very competent students from another class.

However it is set up, it's well worth telling your students what will happen a day or two before you plan to do the interview. Ask them to study the relevant pages of the Student's Book so that they have time to absorb the scenario and think about their part and the language they might need.

The questions aim to be challenging. Questions of the 'Where do you live?'/'How many brothers and sisters have you got?' type have been avoided because students at this level find them to unstimulating, especially when asked by the person they have been friends with for the last five years! However, it's worth letting them know that questions of this type are used in the warm-up phase of the exam.

On the day the interview is to be carried out, it's a good idea to refresh students' minds by organising them into a 'journalists' and an 'interviewees' group and going over the content areas and language points.

With the journalists group, you may choose to drill the question forms briefly and help students decide which of the prompts to include on their list. Elicit ideas of possible answers they might get in the interview and other prompts they'd like to use.

The interviewees have to use a variety of coping strategies. The functional language includes dealing with personal questions, being flexible/adapting questions and showing you need thinking time. It addresses the comments made by examiners (and by interviewers in general) about the difficulties of understanding how an interviewee is feeling, e.g. 'Is that blank look incomprehension or are they just taking time to think?', 'Has what I said offended culturally or prodded old wounds?'

It's helpful to drill the functional language with students and to check their understanding of its appropriateness, especially in relation to dealing with personal questions, which is a culturally loaded area.

Students will probably need examples of how they can adapt questions. You should offer prompts, such as 'I'm afraid I don't know much about my parents, but I can talk about my sister, who I live with now' or 'I can't tell you much about a community project which improved neighbourhood facilities, but I can tell you about a project I was involved in to get a coffee bar at school.' Obviously, the adaptation has to be sensibly related to the original question asked by the interviewer/examiner.

In relation to the exam, it's useful to remind students that the oral examiner is looking for the ability to sustain a reasoned conversation with facts, examples and anecdotal information.

4 Honest feedback

Analysis of the success of the interview is invaluable in helping students achieve greater ease and fluency. Getting to grips with one's own interview skills effectively is tough, however, even for native speakers. Remind students that interviews are a process, not a product. Your own observation of the role play will, of course, provide you with ideas of what your particular group needs.

The following examples give ideas of what often goes wrong in interviews. The remarks encapsulate the criteria against which students are judged in the oral assessment. Why not ask students to identify the underlying problems in the examples and how they could be overcome? You can use your knowledge of the class to adapt the examples to what actually happened.

I would have talked for longer if you hadn't been yawning/shuffling papers. (body language)

I would have felt more comfortable in the interview if you hadn't kept asking me about pets when I had told you we don't have any. (flexibility)

I would have been able to give better answers if you'd let me think about the question a bit longer. (allowing time for answers)

Most of your answers were just one or two words. It was very hard to get the conversation going fluently. I needed detail in your answers to be able to choose the follow-up questions. (communication)

I had to keep asking you to repeat what you said because I couldn't understand you the first time. (pronunciation)

You kept using the wrong words or missing words out. I couldn't always understand what you meant. (lexis)

Students are asked to make a note of what they want to remember for next time, e.g. *Next time I'll think more about my body language/try to give more complete answers/try to give examples/use more open questions/listen more carefully/work at developing my vocabulary.*

5 Reading

The text, from The *Times* Saturday magazine, is about Diane Modahl, a well-known black British athlete. The article is appealing and useful because the writer's 'hand' is almost invisible. By using Diane's words and letting incidents speak for themselves, the writer conveys a natural portrait of the athlete.

ANSWERS

a 4   **b** 3   **c** 2   **d** 5   **e** 1

6 Discussion

Straight after the first reading, it's revealing to ask students what they thought of the journalist's interview skills. You can ask *'Do you think the writer has been successful in getting Diane to talk freely about herself? How do you think he or she did this?'*

7 Detailed comprehension

ANSWERS

1   He organised sports days for the children in the neighbourhood.
2   It was much bigger and it was situated in a white, middle-class area.
3   She felt a bit nervous but she looked forward to it because she was confident in her ability as a runner.
4   She took the girls' remarks calmly and at face value.
5   *Possible answer*
    Diane has a very strong relationship with her husband, Vicente, and they depend greatly on each other. She feels meeting him has helped her grow up. She is more confident about leaving her home town and trying new things. She feels it is possible for her to achieve any ambition if she decides to pursue it. She wants to set a positive example for their child. *(66 words)*

VOCABULARY: ANSWERS

a   bemused *(line 48)*
b   siblings *(line 1)*
c   marinated *(line 10)*

d stands for (*line 13*)
e inadvertent (*line 43*)
f relished (*line 67*)
g contemplated (*line 72*)
h blatant (*line 49*)
i the Pied Piper (*line 21*) In this well-known, rather haunting story, a small town becomes overrun with rats. Officials employ a rat catcher who rids the town of the rats. They then refuse to pay him. The Pied Piper takes his revenge by playing his pipe which attracts all the children of the town. The children follow him to a magical cave and disappear forever.

8 Describing Diane

ANSWERS

single-minded, good-natured, sociable, sporty, adventurous

9 Describing Diane's family

ANSWERS

exuberant – high-spirited
critical – judgmental
close-knit – supportive
go-ahead – dynamic
reticent – reserved
hospitable – welcoming
down-to-earth – ordinary

The adjectives which best describe Diane's family are: close-knit/supportive, go-ahead/dynamic, hospitable/welcoming, down-to-earth/ordinary.

It's very fruitful at this stage to spend a little time analysing the way the reader's impressions of Diane are formed. Students will have drawn their own conclusions about Diane's family from a wide variety of textual clues. It's interesting to make this process more conscious. What we know is largely inferred, and we piece together the clues to get a complete picture.

You could ask *'What makes you think her family are supportive?'* A student might say 'I don't know exactly why, I just feel that they are, probably, from the way they live.' This would be a good answer and you could follow it up by exploring the underlying meaning of Diane's comment (lines 81-4) that her parents wouldn't hold her back (they are proud of her and want her to achieve all she can, even if it means seeing less of her). You can elicit other ideas which reinforce the concept of supportiveness, e.g. she always feels home is a place that she can go back to; the way their parents worked to give their children a better start.

10 Colloquial words

ANSWERS

broke (have no money)
paper (newspaper)
conned (cheated)

on the blink (not working properly – usually of something mechanical)
a bit dodgy (rather unreliable)
stroppy (awkward, bad-tempered)
crook (criminal)
quid (pounds)

It's well worth asking students about the advantages of using colloquial words (they sound friendly, they help you seem more fluent if you use them in conversation) and disadvantages (they sometimes don't have a very precise meaning, it's hard to know quite how you can use them, it can be difficult to know when a word is colloquial or slang).

11 Translation

Check with students which colloquial words they like using in their own language(s) and ask them to suggest some equivalents for the words in the passage.

12 Discussion

Encourage students to make links in the discussion between home and family life and the kind of person you eventually turn out to be. You may like to consider cultural attitudes to family duties and responsibilities. You could ask *'How much do children owe their parents?'* It's also interesting to hear students' ideas on the support and inspiration they can receive from outside the family circle.

As students will be considering cultural ideas about families later in the unit, this is an opportunity to check *'How far does Diane's family conform to your notion of a typical English family?'* Try to establish exactly how and why they think they are similar or different. You could go beyond colour to consider the large size of the family, its easy-going warmth, its lack of reserve, etc.

This could lead on to an interesting discussion about the supposed characteristics of different nationalities (are all people from the Caribbean warm and jolly?, are all English people reserved?, etc) and how we come to form ideas about what people from other countries are like (e.g. historical reasons/media/folklore/lack of direct knowledge and contact).

13 Idioms

ANSWERS

1 You have more obligations to someone when there is a blood relationship.
2 People related to you be blood. The expression is usually used by parents referring to their children.
3 It pays enough to keep us out of serious financial trouble.

Favourite places

14 Discussion

The discussion focuses students' thoughts on the new topics.

The aim of the following sequence of exercises is to encourage subjective, descriptive writing of a favourite place, giving reasons for the choice. The only guidelines are that it has to be real, not imaginary, set, roughly speaking, in the student's locality, and that it should be a place for which they feel genuine enthusiasm – not just a place they feel they *should* like. The IGCSE exam rewards fresh, original writing which provides unusual glimpses of what the students really like in their locality. If, in addition, they are able to give thoughtful, appropriate reasons for their choice, they can attract the highest marks.

One of the challenges for students will be working out what exactly is appealing about a familiar place and explaining its effect on their mood. It doesn't matter how ordinary the place is (a local park, a nearby patch of woods). Remind them this is a personal piece of writing, not a tourist brochure description – although it could be adapted for this later.

(The photograph shows a typical scene in the Pennine Hills in northern England.)

15 Reading and vocabulary

You'll probably want to spend some time working on this preparatory exercise. It involves reading a personal description of a market, and deciding which categories the adjectives and descriptive phrases belong to. You should check with students whether the market appeals to them and ask why/why not, to give them practice in explaining their reasons.

16 Writing

Before they begin to write a draft description of their own favourite place, encourage students to do the visualisation exercise which will help them recall the place in detail and the feelings it evokes.

The actual writing might be best done for homework. Emphasise that dictionaries will be essential.

17 Reading aloud

It is a good idea to keep the written pieces anonymous, for the sake of more self-conscious students. Encourage students to respond warmly to the descriptions they hear, giving reasons why they would enjoy the place too. This will foster the spirit which makes all the difference to group dynamics.

18 Showing enthusiasm

 Remind students that appropriate stress and intonation are vital if you are to convince your listener you are genuinely enthusiastic. Point out that the voice jumps to a higher pitch at the beginning of the stressed words and then falls.

GRAMMAR NOTES

Point out to students that they are using **what** + noun or noun phase:
What a great place! I think my friends and I would love the atmosphere there!
What fun! My younger brothers and sisters would love it!

or **how** + adjective:
How exciting! It would be a fascinating place for my friends and I to go at weekends.
How relaxing! It'd be a wonderful place for me to unwind after studying all day.

TAPESCRIPT

As in the Student's Book.

19 Order of adjectives

Remind students that numbers usually go before adjectives, e.g. *two large eggs*.

Commas are generally used between longer adjectives and in longer sequences, especially where a slight pause would be made in speech.

As three adjectives before the noun are usually enough, students practise putting this number of adjectives into order.

ANSWERS

1 I've lost a red canvas sports bag.
2 We stayed in a quaint, three-bedroomed, Swedish house.
3 The new boss is a friendly, middle-aged, Egyptian woman.
4 I want to buy a good-quality, black leather jacket.
5 I've bought a warm tweed winter coat.
6 Thieves stole a priceless, oriental silver teapot.
7 On holiday I enjoyed trying the tasty, Indian vegetarian food.
8 How do you remove coffee stains from an expensive, Chinese silk rug?

20 Developing a more mature style

Clauses are used to give information in descriptions. They sound more natural than using a long sequence of adjectives before the noun, and create a more graceful style.

PRACTICE: ANSWERS

1 He gave her an unusual Russian box made of wood with a picture of a famous story on the lid. (*or* ... an unusual Russian wooden box)
2 She was wearing a brown wool suit which looked too warm for the weather.
3 It's a white, Japanese, portable television with a hundred channels.
4 It's a heavy, French, copper frying pan with a lid.
5 Someone's taken my blue pottery coffee mug with my name on it.

6 He has lost a grey polyester school coat with/which has his name on the inside.
7 Rosanna decided to wear a long, green-and-white, silk dress which she had bought in America.

What do teenagers want?

The listening exercise is based on a typical IGCSE scenario: a disused warehouse is up for conversion. Should it be turned into a study centre or a youth club? Why? A dialogue takes place between two officials. Pamela has looked through the letters about the conversion from local teenagers and is in favour of a study centre. John, her colleague, prefers the idea of a youth club.

21 Discussion

Prepare students first by asking them to talk about any community initiatives they may have taken part in, and let them explain the difficulties they faced and their feelings (frustration, pride, etc). If it's more appropriate, you could make this discussion more school based, and ask them if they have been involved in making improvements at school (e.g. getting a common room).

Extend the discussion to consider the improvements they would like to see in their own neighbourhood.

22 Before you listen: Vocabulary check

ANSWERS

maintenance: keeping something in good condition
facilities: buildings or services provided for a particular purpose
wear and tear: the effect of repeated use
drain on resources: using up too much money
budget: a spending plan; to make such a plan
voluntary: (working) without pay
premises: a piece of land and its buildings

23 Listening for gist

 As always, it's a good idea to listen once for the main ideas and to check basic understanding. Replay the tape, pausing it in places if necessary.

ANSWERS

1 She wants a study centre.
2 He wants a youth club.
3 'When you put it like that, maybe ...'

TAPESCRIPT

Listen to the conversation for general meaning first, and find answers to the three questions.

PAMELA: Right, John, I've put all the letters we received with unsuitable or impractical ideas over there for you to look through later if you like. Two ideas really stood out. The idea of converting the warehouse into a study centre for after-school studies was very popular. Also very popular was the request for a social club, a sort of youth club.

JOHN: What do you want to go for?

P: I'm all in favour of converting it into a study centre. It would be very cheap to run because it wouldn't need much maintenance. Students could come after school and at weekends to do homework or research school projects. As a lot of them are sharing bedrooms at home, they have nowhere suitable to study.

J: But Pamela, do you really think it's a good idea to develop it as a study centre? After all, we already have an excellent public library, only five minutes away. What's wrong with that?

P: But it's always crowded! The staff are rushed off their feet with all they have to do and they aren't very helpful to students.

J: A study centre sounds all right in theory, but in practice it's not going to solve the very real problem of the lack of leisure facilities for teenagers.

P: I take your point, John, but qualifications are very important if they're to do well in the future. Isn't it up to us to help them?

J: Oh, talking about the future is all very well, but what about the present? Teenagers who aren't interested in studying don't want a study centre. Having a youth club would be fun for everyone. They all deserve a place where they can unwind after a long day at school or work.

P: Well, I'm not absolutely convinced. I think parents would prefer a study centre much more than they want a rowdy and undisciplined youth club.

J: We can't know what parents want because they haven't been asked. I don't think young people will be rowdy. Most of them are well behaved. Just think of how hard local teenagers work to raise money for disabled people in the town.

P: Well, I think it's rather unrealistic to expect no noise or litter or wear and tear. In my view, a youth club is going to be expensive to maintain. It'll be a drain on resources.

J: Well, I accept that a youth club will be more expensive to maintain than a study centre. We could reduce maintenance costs and control misbehaviour by having a supervisor in charge.

P: Can we afford a supervisor?

J: I've had a look at the budget and it would stretch to paying a small wage for the first year of the club's operation. After that we'd have to review it. Even consider voluntary help.

P: Hmmm. Not many people want to work for nothing.

J: And we shouldn't forget that the premises are next to a sports field, so there's no worry about a lot of noise late at night. (Well,) it's not as if it's in a residential street.

P: That's true, but you never know, do you? I still say a study centre is the better bet.

J: Well, look at it this way: what's worse – a youth club or the situation of young people hanging around the streets at night? Do you remember that awful case in the papers recently?

P: Oh, that was a tragedy!

J: It was said those teenagers would be alive today if they'd had a decent place to spend their free time.

P: Yes, I remember that.

J: I know we both feel the safety of young people comes first.

P: I agree with you there.

J: A well-run youth club could put many people's minds at rest.

P: Hmmm. When you put it like that, maybe a youth club isn't such a bad idea after all.
J: So you're willing to give it a try?
P: Only if a proper supervisor is taken on.
J: Oh great! I'll let the Social Committee know. Well, let's keep our fingers crossed they give the idea the go-ahead.

24 Detailed listening

 Let students listen again for detail and to find the answers to the true/false exercise.

ANSWERS

1	false
2	true
3	true
4	true
5	true
6	true
7	false
8	false
9	true
10	false

25 Follow-up

Let students discuss their feelings about the youth club versus study centre freely. How they feel will naturally depend a lot on their own cultural background and the opportunities they have around them.

IDIOMS

The idioms 'I'm digging my heels in' and 'I'm sticking to my guns' could be applied equally to John or Pamela, as neither wants to give in.

26 Persuading: Stress and intonation

 This further listening to the dialogue focuses on the intonation of informal persuasion. The phrases have a generally falling pattern. Before starting the exercise, it may be interesting to find out from students which phrases they now use when they want to change someone's mind.

Make sure students can complete the phrases appropriately, e.g.

Do you REALLY think it's a good idea *to encourage teenagers to stay out at night?*

That's true, BUT *not everyone will enjoy it.*

That's all very well, BUT *other things are more important.*

Monitor their stress and intonation.

TAPESCRIPT

As in the Student's Book.

27 Role play: Spend, spend, spend

Role plays are a good opportunity to practise functions and intonation in a more spontaneous context. Here students imagine they are part of a family of four (mum, dad, two teenage children) that has won £10,000 in a competition. Each student aims to persuade the others that his/her ideas are the best way of spending the money for the benefit of the whole family.

Students could recycle some of the language they heard on the tape, e.g. *I'm all in favour of ...* . It's good to remind them, however, that role plays work best when they use all the language resources at their command without being too self-conscious or too inhibited. Emphasise the fact that the need to communicate overrides worrying about accurate grammar or vocabulary.

Divide students into groups of four. Allow them a few minutes to absorb the details of their roles before starting, and clarify any misunderstandings. Why not take a back seat during the role play and leave feedback for later?

Living with a foster family

28 Pre-reading discussion

It will be interesting to see how students respond to the concept of fostering, which has many cultural implications. In the UK, the foster family option is considered by social workers for children whose own families cannot look after them and there are no relatives who could help. It is considered preferable to putting a child into a children's home. Children can be fostered for a few weeks or many years.

Before they begin reading, you could ask students to discuss the sort of problems which might lead to fostering (death of a parent, financial troubles, illness).

Your students might be very keen on the idea of a foster brother or sister (more companionship, the pleasure of getting to know a new person) or find it threatening (more sharing, possibly more stress in the house, less attention from parents, etc). It will be fascinating to hear their views.

29 Reading for gist

ANSWERS

Craig is being fostered because his widowed mother was having problems coping. Yes, he's happy.

30 Vocabulary

ANSWERS

1E 2A 3D 4C 5G 6F 7B

31 Post-reading discussion

The aim of this exercise is to equip students to use clues in the style of the writing to identify an author's main aim. Encourage students to back up their choices with examples from the text.

ANSWERS

Author's main aim: b

Structure: a

Style: chatty

32 Comprehension check

ANSWERS

1 They have three children.
2 They had a family discussion and asked the children what they thought.
3 The fostering liaison officer and the head of year at the school have been very helpful.
4 Adapting to different rules – he now helps clear up after meals and says where he is going.
5 *Possible answer*
   Rita is a good foster mother because she does not try to take the place of Craig's real mother. She lets him talk about his feelings and tries to understand him. She stays calm when family life is hectic, and she gives Craig affection and reassurance.

You could round off the exercise asking students whether they think fostering is a good idea and what they think the Dawson family have gained from fostering Craig.

33 Further discussion

The discussion could explore ideas along the following lines.

A The idea that fostered children are troublemakers is largely a fantasy of the media. You might guess that someone is a troublemaker through aggressive body language, verbal comments, a style of dress which is inappropriate for an occasion, etc. On the other hand, many teenagers are labelled 'troublemakers' simply because they do not conform to conventional expectations of dress and appearance, but their behaviour is not actually disruptive or threatening.

B **Advantages of fostering through informal arrangements made by relatives:**
The child's cultural and social identity may be better maintained because of shared backgrounds.

The foster family may be more local for the child.

Disadvantages:
The selection criteria for the foster family may not be very objective.

Advantages of fostering through an official agency:
The selection criteria will probably be more objective and meet stringent regulations.

The foster family will usually receive financial aid from the government or fostering agency.

Disadvantages:
There will probably be lots of red tape.

The child may be placed with a foster family with whom he/she has little in common, far away from his/her local area.

You could expand the discussion to consider whether biological ties with the child's birth family should be broken when a child is fostered (this is common in some countries), or whether it is important for the child to maintain links with his birth parents. In certain countries, many people do not see any difference between adoption and fostering. Students could be asked for their opinion on this too.

34 Colloquial language in context

This exercise will further develop students' grasp of colloquial language. They need to try to identify the meaning of the colloquial expressions in context rather than find exactly similar expressions.

ANSWERS

1 in their house/living with them
2 difficult bureaucratic hurdles
3 in great and searching detail
4 problematic times
5 as if no-one understood or was responding to me
6 without hesitation

EXTENSION IDEAS

Craig's story is quite dramatic in its own way and lends itself well to stimulating creative writing. You could ask students to write the dialogue between Craig and his real mother after his first day with the Dawsons and then to perform it.

You could consider asking students to describe the day Craig came to live with the Dawsons from the point of view of one of the Dawson children. This could be in the form of a letter to a friend or a diary entry.

35 Spelling: Doubling consonants when adding suffixes

Doubling the consonant in one syllable and multi-syllable words presents lots of problems for students and is a very common source of errors. Studying the rules and patterns will deepen students' awareness of language as an orderly system, and is an ideal opportunity to revise and expand their understanding of how affixation alters word meaning and function.

Unfortunately, the rules are complex, but if they are presented to students in the context of developing a broader grasp of overall language patterns, students should quickly appreciate the value of the exercise. Encourage them to be on the look-out for links between spelling, grammar and word stress. Probably the easiest and most dependable rule for students to remember is: *one vowel + one consonant = double consonant.*

PRACTICE: ANSWERS

1 ringing
2 hottest
3 stopped
4 enjoyed
5 saddest
6 shopping
7 chatting
8 walking
9 sending
10 cheaper
11 waiting
12 asking
13 looking
14 swimming
15 rocky

36 Adding suffixes to multi-syllable words

PRACTICE: ANSWERS

1 regretted
2 permitted
3 occurred
4 reasoned
5 committed
6 happened
7 explained, beginning
8 preferred

37 Look, say, cover, write, check

Students undoubtedly benefit from using a visual strategy to strengthen their recall of spellings. Extra practice with this trustworthy method particularly supports students who do not have a strong visual memory and those who find it difficult to recognise patterns in language.

38 Words from different languages

English is crammed with historical associations and, if they have access to etymological dictionaries, students will enjoy investigating the languages/ places of origin of many common English words. It is interesting to discuss how they came into the language (through colonisation, settlers bringing new words, the French and Viking invaders, etc). There are many stories behind words to whet students' appetite for further discovery. For example, *kindergarten* literally means 'children's garden' in German. The idea comes from the nineteenth-century philosophy of a man who thought that young children were like tender plants which need nurturing to grow.

Other examples to investigate are *zero* (Arabic), *bandit* (Italian), *boomerang* (Australia/aboriginal), *yacht* (Dutch) and *slogan* (a Scottish war cry).

ANSWERS

Arabic:	sofa
Aztec:	chocolate
Chinese:	tea
French:	cuisine
Greek:	athlete
Hindi:	bungalow
Italian:	opera
Japanese:	karate
Latin:	villa
Norwegian:	ski
Persian:	caravan
Spanish:	patio

Welcoming an exchange visitor

This sequence of exercises focuses on achieving an appropriate tone and register when welcoming an exchange visitor to one's home. Achieving a suitable tone is basic to effective communication but a frustratingly difficulty skill to acquire. The exercises will equip students with a range of techniques for hitting the right note.

39 Reassuring your guest

It's a good idea to check first that students understand the concept of an exchange visit. Students of foreign languages, for example, often take turns staying with each other's families. It's an inexpensive way to have a holiday in a foreign country and to find out more about the culture and practise the language. This topic is culturally quite loaded and presents an excellent opportunity to share cultural information about how guests etc are normally treated.

A good starting point before students make their notes is to ask them to see the exchange visit from the point of view of their guest. Elicit the fact that the guest will probably be a bit apprehensive, and then discuss ways of making him/her feel at home. Encourage students to think of the most attractive aspects of their home and surroundings, eliciting a few specific examples, before they write their own notes.

BEGINNINGS AND ENDINGS

The second part of the exercise asks students to select an appropriate beginning and ending. Beginning and ending letters continues to present difficulties for IGCSE students. In English, as in many languages, there are set ways to do this, perhaps because even native speakers find it difficult.

Let students explain why they have rejected the phrases. Only e and **h** are appropriate. The others are unsuitable for cultural reasons and because of ambiguity.

After they have completed this exercise, you may choose to give students a few extra beginning and ending phrases to memorise.

Informal beginnings:
It was lovely to get your last letter.
Many thanks for your last letter.
Just a line to let you know …

Informal endings:
That's all for now.
Do write soon.
Looking forward to hearing from you.
Don't forget to drop me a line.

40 Model letter

The model letter aims to show a straightforward way of describing one's home and locality. One of the biggest challenges for IGCSE candidates continues to be getting the tone and register right. A letter of this type should sound welcoming and the plans/places described should sound inviting.

The format exercise asks students to work out exactly how this effect is achieved. You could point out that the letter gets straight on with the topic. A common complaint about IGCSE candidates is that they fail to get to grips with the topic quickly enough.

41 Achieving a suitable tone

This exercise asks students to analyse examples of tone and register from students' real letters. Ask them if they think the sentences sound right for a letter of welcome. Weaker students, in particular, are going to need time to think carefully about the impression some of these remarks will make on the recipient. To make this clearer, before they begin the exercise, you could put extreme examples on the board and ask students to discuss them. For example: *When you come you'll find awful things about my home, e.g. there is no public transport after 6 p.m., my mum's cooking is terrible, my dad is so strict, my little sister is always annoying me, there is nothing interesting to do.*

Ask *'Does this actually need to be mentioned? What effect will it have?'* Don't forget to remind students that all the things which are boringly familiar to them can sound wonderfully exciting to a complete stranger! If students feel an idea ought to be mentioned, you can discuss ways of presenting the information more positively.

It's more stimulating if students work in pairs to discuss the extracts from the letters because of the need to bounce ideas off each other. It's particularly helpful if you can pair up students from different cultures.

REWRITING

When students have done the pairwork, they can consolidate their learning by rewriting a few sentences with a more appropriate tone. They can have fun choosing sentences and altering the tone and register.

42 Correcting mistakes

The first and final sentences are inappropriate in tone. The first sentence can be omitted. The letter falls into three paragraphs plus a separate closing sentence. Encourage students to keep redrafting until they have come up with an accurate version.

MODEL ANSWER

Dear William,

Thank you for your kindness during the visit I made to your family last month. I have many happy memories of your family, especially your mother. She is the best cook in the world!

I was very surprised by your town. It is extremely pleasant and not as industrial as I expected. I also liked your neighbours, and I won't forget the friendly college students. I enjoyed the activities we did, and I will send you the best photographs of our camping trip in my next letter.

Please come for a holiday with my family. Our house stands by/is next to/is near a lake. My father will let you borrow his little boat. The beaches here are wonderful, and now it is nearly summer so we can go swimming, which I know you enjoy. On cloudy days we can visit some huge shopping centres/malls which are very popular with tourists.

Looking forward to hearing from you. *(or a similar expression)*

Love,
Jacob

43 Sentence completion

This exercise gives students further practice in presenting their home environment positively. You may like to extend it by asking them to write a couple of sentences about their home town using the same pattern, e.g. *Although there is a lot of traffic where we live, we are within walking distance of the shops, cafés and leisure centre.*

REASSURANCE

It's fun for students to share their ideas about how people give reassurance in their language and culture.

44 Surprise party: Tone and register

Students revise and reinforce their understanding of tone and register. The best answer is 3; the others sound aggressive and abrupt in writing.

45 Re-ordering

Students find problem solving fun. This is an ideal exercise to do in pairs or groups of three.

ANSWERS

The order of the letter is as follows, although some variation is possible:

1n	2i	3e	4k	5a	6o	7f	8c	9j
10h	11b	12l	13m	14d	15g			

46 Writing

Students now have an opportunity to put into practice the skills they have developed in the unit.

INTERNATIONAL OVERVIEW

Some people are afraid that the emphasis on English language acquisition in many countries will deprioritise time and attention for local languages, their history and literature. Some say it could affect the syntax of their own languages. For example, Swedish now makes plurals by adding -s. English words are regularly adopted into other languages – Japanese is said to have 20,000 words of English origin, e.g. *remon* for lemon, *hamu* for ham.

After eliciting students' opinions on the good and bad points of the growth of the English language, you could ask them to draw a bar chart to illustrate the 'top' five languages in the world, or shade these areas on a map of the world, if you have time.

Many experts believe that bilingualism helps general intellectual development. You could ask students whether they share this view, and why. Experts also believe that the way people feel about speaking more than one language depends on the attitudes other people have to those languages. This is interesting to explore as it has many implications. You could ask whether students think English is a desirable language to learn and why, and how English compares in this respect with other languages.

WIDER PRACTICE

1 If you have access to English-speaking TV, you could video tape an interview from a chat show. These contain superb real-life examples of functions, e.g. evasion of awkward questions, expressing regrets, praising, commiserating, offering congratulations. Pause the tape in places to let students home in on a particular function. It's particularly nice if you can find a personality students are keen on.

2 For more work on confidence building and demystifying interviews, students could interview local people to find out their feelings about the neighbourhood and its facilities. Retired people often have a little more time and can tell students how life in the locality has changed. Community officials could be interviewed about how the work they do benefits groups in the community. Interviews which are carried out in the first language can be translated into English for report back in class.

3 Short role plays can give further practice in use of register and functional language. The following are some possibilities:

You have to decline an invitation to your friend's party. What do you say?

You have been invited to stay for a week with people you don't know very well. You want to know the house rules. What do you say?

Your friend wants you to babysit but you want to go to bed early that night. What do you say?

4 Language has a fascinating history. Students could research a project on one of its many aspects. For example, the history and development of handwriting is extremely rewarding to investigate. They could find out more about the intriguing stories behind the world's many scripts and present an informative talk to the class.

EXAMPLES OF LIKELY EXAM GRADING

Dear Ali,

I'm happy to her that were going to exchange visit with our familys. I'm fed up of them becous they want me to do things that I don't want to do. Any way they are nice and caind sometimes. you will get to now them. I live in Lodgeton and the area I live in is picfull and quit. You will have a lot of sleep. In the summer you can go to the beach and have fun jetsking etc. The best places I think that is worth visiting is Pizza Club. It's a resturant with a lout of people. bring what ever you want to bring. I'm waiting for your answer,

Your frind.

The positive points of this letter include an attempt to provide information and detail about the writer's background. It communicates in a limited sense. Its lack of paragraphing, obvious structural weakness, spelling and punctuation errors, as well as inappropriate register, would mean that this type of answer would be awarded an E.

Dear Kathleen,

I'm glad that you're soon coming to stay with us! I'm writing you this time just to tell you more about my family, friends, places to see and all that stuff.

To begin with, let me tell you that I live with my parents and a small brother (though he is 10 he won't bother us). Our house is near my school, that means we will not have to wake up very early; you'll also find a cinema next to it, so after we study, we can go see a good film and relax.

I've planned some activities for you to do mostly at the weekends, such as going to museums (interesting ones of course), roller-skating, visiting other nice monuments (the Eiffel Tower for example) among other things. Well that's all for today.

Good luck in your trip!

Kisses,

This letter demonstrates a good tone, style, vocabulary, paragraphing and general organisation. It sounds welcoming and the activities sound inviting. It is work of good quality without displaying any outstanding sophistication. This sort of writing would receive a low to medium B grade.

Sport and Fitness

OVERVIEW

This unit deals with note-taking and summarising. Summarising is tested on both Papers 1 and 2. Note-taking is tested only on Paper 2.

SUMMARISING

The challenges of summarising for students are:

- reshaping the text in their own words while preserving its original meaning
- discriminating between what is relevant to the summary question and what is irrelevant
- connecting the summary grammatically
- keeping to a word limit.

Like the other exam questions, the summary is marked for communicative competence as well as language usage. IGCSE candidates need to show that they have genuinely understood the text and can restate it. Slight grammar and vocabulary errors are of no great importance as long as they do not affect the meaning.

Candidates are asked to write summaries that are no longer than 100 words. Students should aim to keep to this word length to get the highest marks.

There is a lot of evidence to suggest that IGCSE candidates tend to plunge into the summary without going through the essential sequence of steps. The unit emphasises getting the right mental attitude before beginning to read the summary text. This means using textual clues, predicting content and the writer's intention, and recalling information.

Students often find doing summaries on their own a struggle. Pairwork has been incorporated into the exercises at each stage to check accuracy and for mutual support.

NOTE-TAKING

A good note-taking answer in the exam will use a note-form that is clear, understandable and able to be followed by someone who has not seen the original passage. In the exam, bullet points are sometimes given to aid presentation. If these are not given, students should use headings and numbered points where possible. Unlike the summary question, students are not instructed to keep to a word limit, nor are they told to use their own words in their notes. However, the notes should be brief and concise. The best answers tend to have some words and phrases of similar meaning to those used in the text. Candidates must try to avoid copying out chunks of text.

Note-taking from a text is an easier task for candidates than summarising. In this unit, it is treated as one of the stages in producing an effective summary. Students are asked to make notes from a text and then join the notes into a connected summary. Or they are asked to write a set of notes on a passage and then to correct mistakes in a summary of the same text. Note that in the exam different texts are given for note-taking and summary writing.

GUIDED NOTES AND SUMMARIES

In the exam, candidates are often asked to make notes from or summarise a text from a particular angle, rather than writing a general summary or producing a set of notes covering all the main points.

For example, in previous years candidates have been asked to write about *the advantages and disadvantages of … / trace the history of … / outline the causes and effects of … / describe the main facts known about … / explain the best methods of …*.

This is the approach taken to summary and note-taking in the unit.

PARAGRAPH-LENGTH SUMMARY

A paragraph-length guided summary is set at the end of a comprehension passage for Extended candidates (Paper 2, Part 2, exercise 1). This also presents fewer problems for students. The skills for this exercise are subsumed into the general summary skills.

THEME

The theme of sport and its role in education runs throughout the unit. In addition, there is a discussion and summary passage on the importance of diet in keeping us fit. These are popular exam topics and should strike a chord with your students' prior knowledge and experiences.

The texts chosen come from newspapers and magazines. Discussion is slanted to raise issues such as:

- Is competitive sport a good idea for young children?
- How do you interest children in learning a complicated sport?
- Should boxing return to the school curriculum?
- Do diet and fitness programmes prepare us for a healthier life or make us neurotic about food and our shape?

You could also expect this kind of topic in the extended writing questions or in the oral assessment.

LANGUAGE WORK

Specific language exercises focus on ways of writing more concisely, e.g. using compound nouns and noun phrases, finding an exact word instead of a phrase and avoiding unnecessary repetition. There is also work on analysing headlines. 'Newspaper-speak' is a fascinating topic in itself. Headlines, in particular, are short-cuts into the meaning of a text. While difficult, they are well worth trying to understand.

Spelling focuses on a common problem: whether to drop or retain the final *-e* when adding a suffix.

Is sport always fun?

1 Note-taking and summaries: Sharing ideas

Encourage an open discussion about what students like or dislike about summarising and what they find difficult. (Don't be too surprised by negative feedback!) It's nice to point out, if you can, the strengths they are already demonstrating in their approach to summarising. Lots of IGCSE students find the summary question daunting and spend the exam time on the comprehension questions or on the essays. Use the discussion as an opportunity to break into their fears of summarising.

You could consolidate this exercise by asking students to make a list of very specific points they need to improve and ways they could help themselves, e.g. using textual clues, underlining the text.

You could begin by asking students to say what are the main differences between notes and summary writing, eliciting the idea that phrases and abbreviations can be used in note-taking, whereas sentences in a summary should be grammatically constructed. Headings and numbered or bullet points can be used in both. Ask them if they use coloured pens or highlighters when they want to mark the main points of a text.

2 Discussion / 3 Quiz

The discussion and quiz set the scene for the topical work in the subsequent exercises. Bring the class together after the quiz to share their views. Hopefully, responses will be diverse and provide an opportunity for students who are pro- or anti- sport to understand each other's viewpoints. It would be a good idea to check key vocabulary now, as the concepts run throughout the chosen texts, e.g. *self-discipline, coordination.*

4 Is sport always fun? / 5 Pre-reading discussion

Encourage students to describe sports day at school. They could say what races they enjoy entering and which they do not like. If they do not have a sports day, they could say if they would like such an event at their school.

6 Predicting content

Remind students that the right mental framework before reading will really help them cope with the time pressures in the exam.

7 Reading with concentration

This text is a bit shorter than many exam texts set for summary writing. Students should find the content provocative and it will provide practice in tracing the development of an argument.

The original headline has been removed from the text to provide a question later.

Before they read the text, you could tell students they'll be 'tested' on its content. Although this is a rather artificial approach to reading comprehension, it will encourage maximum concentration on the detail.

8 Comprehension check

ANSWERS

1 stomach pains, being sick, difficulty sleeping
2 at a large village primary school
3 They fall down on the track.
4 immense pity
5 very enthusiastic
6 an afternoon of team games and a few races for those who want them

FINDING THE MAIN IDEAS

Students should be able to do this exercise quickly and practise their scan reading skills at the same time.

ANSWERS

A4 B3 C5 D2 E1

9 Checking predictions

It's interesting to relate students' pre-reading predictions with the actual content of the text. To reinforce the right mental approach you could ask: *'Do you think predicting the content of the text makes it easier to understand, even if your predictions are proved wrong?'*

10 Choosing a headline

Selecting a headline for the article will help students consider the whole of the writer's argument. Detailed work on headline formation comes later in the unit. Sometimes students opt for a short title such as 'Sports Day'. This may be because they unconsciously think of headlines as short. However, you should ask *'Would that headline tell us about the writer's attitude to sports day?'*

'Mum raps sports day' would be a good choice. 'Games for a laugh' was the original title. Like many headlines, it includes a play on words which is culturally bound. If students are interested, you could explain how this title, which is ironic, is typical of British humour.

You could round off this stage of comprehension by asking students how far they sympathise with the writer's view. You could ask *'Isn't competition an essential ingredient in modern society? Isn't it best that children get used to the idea of winning and losing early on?'* By presenting the issue so starkly, you could lead students to think about the wider implications of competition. You could also contrast the competitive ethos with a more cooperative economic ethos based on sharing and being supportive, reflected in the writer's notions of 'team games'.

11 Note-taking practice

CHECKING KEY WORDS IN AN EXAM QUESTION

Introduce the exercise by telling students of the need to approach note-taking methodically. Many may feel the exercise is 'easy', especially in view of the preparatory work they have done. However, IGCSE students show a tendency to treat notes relatively casually. It's worth pointing out the difference between writing notes for your own benefit and writing them for others. Orderliness and clarity of presentation are important in IGCSE exam answers. The key words in the note-taking question are: *reasons for having a sports day, negative effects on children, a way sports day could be improved*.

UNDERLINING RELEVANT PARTS OF THE TEXT

After students have underlined the relevant parts of the text, do insist they work with a partner to compare notes and clarify any differences. For the pairwork to provide maximum benefit, it's probably best here, as in the rest of the unit, to pair an able student with a less able one.

MAKING NOTES IN YOUR OWN WORDS

Students should try to present their notes in their own words as far as possible. The IGCSE note-taking exercise in the exam doesn't actually specify 'in your own words'. In practice, however, students do need to use some of their own words because, like the summary, the note-taking question tends to be slanted in a particular way e.g. asking students to *advise, evaluate, compare and contrast, give the history of, outline the advantages and disadvantages of*, etc.

For the exam summary question, students always have to write in their own words where they can. Evidence suggests that many IGCSE students move straight from underlining the text at the reading stage to writing the finished draft. If your students do this, they may fall into the trap of 'lifting' (copying) from the text. Such answers fail to demonstrate the comprehension of the material which is vital for a high mark.

12 Comparing two summaries

The 'model' summary versions present very common mistakes which reflect the problems IGCSE students have, e.g. inappropriate linking, failure to use own words, introducing ideas/opinions of one's own. Introducing one's own opinions is a particular problem for IGCSE students when the text is opinion-based. Make sure students do discriminate between the writer's opinion and the 'own ideas' of the model versions.

After students have worked alone or in pairs to compare and contrast the two summary versions, it's nice to draw them together as a class. This is an opportunity to address any queries they have so far with summary writing or note-taking.

ANSWERS

1 Summary 1
2 Summary 2
3 Summary 1. *Moreover* is wrong. A contrast word or phrase is needed, e.g. *On the other hand, Nevertheless, However. Despite* should be *Even.*
4 Each summary introduces, at the end, an opinion which is not mentioned by the writer.
5 Summary 2, because it uses the writer's own words.

Enjoying sports safely

13 Compound nouns

Compound nouns (noun + noun combinations) are common in English and are increasing in number as more new ideas and things are invented. In this exercise, students are asked to identify some commonly-used compound nouns from a possible list.

ANSWERS

The words which commonly follow *sports* are: bag, car, centre, club, equipment, instructor, man, person, woman. Note that, unlike the other compounds, *sportsman, sportsperson* and *sportswoman* are written as one word.

Sports drink is a compound which could be coined if a special drink for sport were invented and widely recognised. You can use this example to talk about the relative flexibility of English.

PRACTICE: ANSWERS

swimming + costume, hat, pool, team, trunks

football + match, players, shorts, team, boots, field, shirt

hockey + match, players, stick, team, boots, field

fitness + programme, centre

skating + costume, programme, rink, team, centre

leisure + programme, centre, shirt

cricket + match, bat, team, field
(*Note:* a cricket player is called a *cricketer.*)

Elicit examples of other compounds students already know and write them on the board. Point out that common compounds consisting of two short words are usually written together, e.g. *postman, toothpaste, timetable.* Hyphenated compounds, e.g. *dry-cleaner's,* are becoming increasingly uncommon.

Compounds usually have the stress on the first syllable. Some compound nouns can be reversible, e.g. *race horse, horse race,* which is a special feature of English thought not to be found in other languages.

14 Pre-listening discussion

The listening exercise asks students to listen to a recorded announcement about a sports centre and complete a diary. The term 'Sports centre' has a culturally specific meaning, so it's wise to check with students that they understand that all kinds of facilities (swimming, squash, aerobics, weight training etc) are usually offered under one roof.

15 Listening to a recorded announcement

 The first part of the exercise builds on the work on compound nouns. First, let students listen for general meaning and to complete the compound nouns on the list. Then they should listen again to fill in the diary.

Re-play the tape as often as you wish.

ANSWERS

1 open-air swimming pool
2 coin-return locker system
3 changing rooms
4 badminton court
5 table tennis
6 cheap-rate tickets
7 sports centre members
8 application form
9 reception desk
10 keep fit classes

SPORTS CENTRE DIARY: ANSWERS

(i) Need 50p coin for lockers.
(ii) Sports centre closed.
(iii) Bring own badminton racquet.
(iv) Ask supervisor for free bats and balls.
(v) Gym open 2-4 p.m.
(vi) Must wear indoor shoes.
(vii) Collect application form from reception desk.
(viii) Senior citizens' keep-fit classes.

Membership of the Sports centre costs £12 for adults and £6 for junior members.

TAPESCRIPT

You are going to hear some recorded information about facilities available at a sports centre. Listen first for general meaning and try to complete the list of compound nouns, putting one word in each space.

On Monday we have swimming in the open-air swimming pool from 9 a.m. to 11 a.m. Please make sure you bring a 50p coin with you as a coin-return locker system has recently been installed in the changing rooms. On Monday afternoon the sports centre is closed. On Tuesday morning the badminton court is available from 10 a.m. to 11.30. Players must use their own badminton racquets. On Tuesday afternoon we are open for schools only. Table tennis is available on Wednesday morning from 9 till 11.30. The bats and balls for the game are supplied free of charge by making a request to the supervisor. The gym is open on Wednesday afternoon from 2 till 4 p.m. It is essential that indoor shoes are worn. Membership of the sports centre is £12 for adults and £6 for junior members. Please note that cheap-rate tickets are available to sports centre members only. If you wish to become a member, please pick up an application form from the reception desk which is open on Thursday mornings. On Thursday afternoons, keep-fit classes especially for senior citizens are held. Please enquire at reception.

16 Marking the main stress

 Stressing words correctly is an important part of conveying meaning. In this exercise, the main stress is marked on words which the speaker wishes to emphasise, to correct any misunderstanding. Give students a few examples before they listen, e.g.

A: *Did you forget your football shorts?*
B: *No, I forgot my boots.*
A: *What did you learn from the coach?*
B: *I learned everything from the coach.*

Ask students to identify where the main stress falls. Ask them *'What is the speaker trying to show by emphasising this word?'*

Now let students listen two or three times to the recorded dialogue and then have them practise by reading aloud in pairs.

TAPESCRIPT

As in Student's Book. Note that in 'Poland plays France every season', the main stress should be marked on 'every'.

PRACTICE: ANSWERS

The key words which should be stressed are: *never, No-one, Everybody, any.*

17 Analysing headlines

Headlines are a fascinating area of English, with a style and grammar of their own. For brevity and dramatic effect they use short words which are uncommon in ordinary language, e.g. *wed* instead of *marry,* or words with unusual meanings, e.g. *bid* for *attempt, rap* for *criticise.*

Being more aware of headlines will help students deal with summarising newspaper articles. The exercises in the Student's Book can give only a 'taste' of newspaper-speak. However, you may like to refer students to *Practical English Usage* by Michael Swan, which has a comprehensive list of headline vocabulary with clear definitions.

You could introduce the topic by bringing in a few headlines from English newspapers to read aloud to the class. This would be especially useful if you could compare the headlines for the same story in different newspapers. If no suitable real headlines are available, write some on the board, e.g. JUDGE RAPS UNREPENTANT BIRD WOMAN, and encourage students to break them down by approaching them in reverse order.

Ask them if 'bird woman' is a regular compound noun or made up for the purpose and what it could mean (a woman who cares for birds). 'Raps' is newspaper-speak for 'criticises'. 'Unrepentant' indicates that the woman has been criticised before and has not followed the judge's orders.

Elicit from students the reasons why newspapers adopt this style. Answers could include: to save space, to be dramatic, to be eye-catching, to be humorous.

Let students complete the exercise in pairs and then check their answers to the exercise in the whole group.

ANSWERS

The key words in the report are: *female student, injured, collision, bus, rejected, compensation.*

18 Expanding headlines

ANSWERS

If rewritten as complete sentences, the headlines might read:

There is hope for the baby who is in a coma because an American surgeon is going to operate on him/her.

A child has been rescued with only minor injuries from a fire on a train.

19 Noun or verb?

This exercise gives more practice with the vocabulary of headlines.

ANSWERS

1/2	aid
3/4	head
5/6	arm
7/8	vow
9/10	cut
11/12	jail

You could extend the exercise by discussing the way the stress shifts in some words depending on whether they are used as a noun or a verb, e.g. *record, reject, produce.*

20 Comparing languages

Why not ask students to bring in examples of headlines in their own language to compare with headlines in English?

21 Discussion

If students are slow in producing ideas about reasons for injuries, you could suggest:

not warming up

not using the right technique

not following the rules

failure to wear protective clothing.

22 Re-wording

As a step towards summary writing, students are asked to put single sentences into their own words. It is interesting to discuss which words can be changed and which words (e.g. technical terms) need to stay the same.

There is no set formula for the alterations. Using active forms is one possible option. You need to encourage students to make the most of all their language resources and to ask themselves: 'Which words in this sentence is it possible to change? Have the changes in structure and vocabulary altered the meaning significantly?'

As students study the example, ask them:

'Is the meaning the same as the original?' (Yes, it is close enough to be perfectly acceptable as a summary.)

'Is it more concise?' (Yes. 'Should' and 'do' are more concise than 'would be well advised' and 'carry out'.)

'Which words haven't been changed and why?' ('Weight training' and 'gym' can't really be changed because there are no concise synonyms.)

When students have completed the exercise, ask for examples of re-wording to compare and contrast among the whole group.

POSSIBLE ANSWERS

1 Many severe injuries cause bleeding and discomfort.
2 For the first day, ice should not be used for more than ten minutes at a time.
3 Never put ice straight onto the skin because it may cause burns.
4 The best treatment for the initial swelling and pain is rest.
5 However, you should start gently moving the injured part as soon as possible.
6 If possible, ask a physiotherapist to supervise any exercise.
7 Drugs from your doctor may help to reduce the pain and swelling of your injury.

23 Writing a short summary

This exercise is not too demanding and you could set it as a timed exercise for your more able students. If you have a weaker group, it will help to build up their confidence. When students have finished, you could ask for help from the whole group in building up a complete version on the board. Draw their attention to the fact that the list of examples of protective equipment should be left out.

POSSIBLE ANSWER

You can avoid sports injuries by using a rational and well-organised approach to training. Do not attempt to train when you are tired, as fatigue can lead to injuries. Ensure that you use good techniques and that you wear protective equipment if necessary, and suitable footwear.

24 Expressing warnings

In this exercise, students practise warning each other about the risks of various sporting activities. You could ask good pairs of students to read the model dialogues aloud to the class. Check understanding of the more specialised vocabulary items, such as *lose coordination* and *run aground*.

PRACTICE

Monitor the mini-conversations to ensure that students are incorporating appropriate warning language. As always, pairs of students who have performed well could be asked to present good dialogues to the rest of the group to round off the exercise.

Additional situations could be:

canoeing/make sure you wear a helmet

skating/watch out for thin ice

swimming/look out for dangerous currents.

Learning cricket

25 Pre-reading discussion

Introduce the topic by asking students their opinions of cricket. If they know the game, you could ask them to talk about whether they found it easier or more difficult to learn than other sports and why. If students don't know anything about cricket, you could make the discussion more general. You could ask, for example, which sports they've found hard to learn but worth the effort.

26 Predicting content

If students are slow in coming up with ideas, you could suggest other points, e.g.

1 how the project is funded
2 children's rate of progress
3 attitudes of the children
4 comments from the teachers
5 comments from the instructors.

27 Vocabulary check

ANSWERS

1B 2A 3D 4C

28 Reading with concentration

The text reflects the exam in length and difficulty. Remind students of the value of combining fast and slow speeds for maximum reading efficiency.

29 True/false comprehension

ANSWERS

1 true 2 false 3 true 4 true 5 true 6 false
7 true 8 true 9 false

30 Checking predictions

Students can't really be told often enough that predicting content is a great way into a quick understanding of a text. This exercise gives them further practice.

31 Writing a headline

Ask students *'What headline would give the reader a good idea of what this text is about?'* Encourage them to apply what they've learned about headlines (strings of nouns, few grammar elements, short words, dramatic effects, use of present tenses). The original headline was 'Kwik way for cricket to catch them young'. If you tell students this, you could point out the play on words implicit in 'Kwik (quick) way' and 'to catch'.

32 Post-reading discussion

To round off the reading exercise, ask students *'Imagine you are able to learn a sport you have never tried before. What would you choose? Why?'*

33 Making notes

Encourage students to approach the note-taking exercise methodically, checking each stage with a partner. It's better to correct inaccuracies when small steps have been completed, rather than getting bogged down when work begins later on correcting a completed summary.

34 Correcting a connected summary

Some students might think correcting a completed summary after making notes is rather overdoing it. However, they need this kind of routine drilling if they are to overcome the summarising hurdles.

The connected summary contains names, jobs, titles, etc which are redundant and should usually be avoided in summaries.

35 Rewriting a summary

MODEL ANSWER

The aim of the project is to encourage young children to take up cricket. The best approach to teaching cricket to young children is to get the children's concentration, keep everyone active and involved, and let all the children have some time to hit the ball. At William Davies School, the project links with the interest children's families, who are largely Asian, already have in cricket. It is also popular because it introduces children to the ideas of teamwork and fair play, and the mental attitudes required to learn a game successfully. *(92 words)*

36 Expressions of measurement

ANSWERS

1 She uses a fifty-minute fitness video.
2 He made a six-inch-deep cut.
3 Ali got a thousand-pound contract.
4 They ordered a six-course meal.
5 I need a ten-pence coin for the phone.
6 It's a ten-minute drive to work.
7 Tanya gave birth to a seven-pound baby.
8 I'd like a two-pound bag of sugar.

Other examples to discuss are:

a two-litre bottle of milk

a fifteen-minute wait

a three-day course.

With a fairly able group, you could extend the exercise by explaining that the plural -*s* is retained when we use 'worth', with the addition of an apostrophe, e.g.

I paid a lot of money for five minutes' worth of help.

He bought three pounds' worth of tokens to use in the machine.

Boxing in schools

37 Pre-reading discussion

Introduce the topic by asking students to look at the photograph and give their opinions of boxing. You could ask *'Do you think it's enjoyable to watch/healthy/highly skilled/has a positive image?'*

The pre-reading tasks are extensive because the text is tough.

38 Vocabulary check

ANSWERS

1F **2**C **3**D **4**B **5**E **6**A

40 Reading with concentration

As always, ask students to read with as much concentration as possible.

41 Audience awareness

POSSIBLE ANSWERS

1 The newpaper has chosen a photo of boxers who could still be of school age.
2 The first sentence of the article mentions a school and then the rest of the article is focused on the effect on school children of the scheme. The views of a PE teacher are quoted.

42 Multiple-choice comprehension

1c **2**c **3**c **4**b **5**c

To round off the comprehension, it would be interesting to ask students about the wider implications of boxing in schools and to explore their views, e.g.

'Will it encourage playground fighting?'

'Do you think the boxing clubs might be rough and encourage bad habits in children?'

'Will young 'boxers' become over-confident about their ability in street fights, etc?'

'Is telling young people about the dangers of boxing much use? Will they assume 'It'll never happen to me?''

43 Writing a for and against summary

Students are gradually given less support to write summaries as they build up their skills and become more confident. However, you may wish to adapt this exercise to your particular group. If you prefer, you could spend a little time asking students to work in groups making a list of points. The list could be checked with the group before students start individual work on the summary. Revise suitable connectors, e.g. *moreover, in addition, however, on the other hand, nevertheless.* Remind students of the need to leave their own ideas out of the summary.

Having students in pairs to check each other's summaries is a methodical way of making sure they have covered all the points.

MODEL ANSWER

You could circulate a copy of the model answer for students to compare with their own. The summary should read something like this:

Schools stopped teaching boxing because it was seen as dangerous. In addition, professional boxing had made a bad impression which was worsened by the death of Bradley Stone. The points in favour of boxing are that it is popular with boys and has improved their skills and sense of self-worth. In addition, progress is easily seen. Moreover, it is a non-contact version so it cannot cause serious injuries. On the other hand, the medical view is that pupils might be encouraged to take up risky contact boxing later. It is argued that other sports teach similar skills without the dangers. *(100 words)*

44 Vocabulary: Using fewer words

This exercise recycles vocabulary items from the reading text.

ANSWERS

1 deprived
2 flourished
3 exacerbated
4 conference
5 unique

45 Redundant words

This exercise will increase students' awareness of a key difference between speech and writing. If possible, bring in a tape lasting about one or two minutes of unedited, completely natural conversation. Ask students to write down exactly what they hear. It's very interesting to analyse the way people really speak, especially with regard to redundancy.

If you aren't able to do this, you could write on the board as an example:
When writing a summary it helps to start by using small steps to begin with.

Ask students which words are repeating the same idea *(start/begin with)*. You could then ask why we tend to repeat ourselves in spoken language, eliciting that this is a strategy to compensate for the transitory nature of speech.

ANSWERS

1 first/begin to
2 's feet
3 old; which are so valuable it is impossible to say how much they are worth
4 unexpected
5 very
6 to cut with
7 saying the same words over and over again
8 unhealthily

46 Spelling: Adding suffixes to words with a final -e

This exercise gives students practice in a very tricky area of spelling. Drawing analogies is one of the best ways of building up knowledge of spelling and vocabulary. Encourage students to make intelligent guesses about why the final *-e* is kept or dropped when a suffix is added. It's an opportunity to make the most of their understanding of word formation.

Keeping or dropping the *-e* basically depends on whether a vowel or consonant suffix is added: consonant suffixes keep the *-e*; vowel suffixes drop it. As you might expect, however, there are numerous exceptions, which is one of the reasons students find this spelling rule rather treacherous.

English is said to have one of the most inconsistent spelling systems of any language, due to its wide variety of language influences over history. It's a fascinating subject, which you may like to explore a little further with your students.

Students can be surprisingly persevering with the intricacies of English spelling. Many feel that the problematic spelling is balanced out by a relatively uncomplicated grammar and the flexibility it allows in word formation, e.g. turning nouns into verb, adjectives and adverbs.

PRACTICE: ANSWERS

education
having
exciting
dancing
creativity
movements
introduction
motivation
stimulating
participating
encouragement
achieving
celebration
stylish
diversity
imaginative

You might like to develop the exercise by exploring some of the possibilities in the other lexical items, e.g. *festive* and *festivity(ies)* linked to *festival*.

47 Word building

1 timing, timely
2 concentrating, concentration
3 refining, refinement
4 exercising
5 welcoming
6 involving, involvement
7 aching
8 stately, statement
9 uniquely, uniqueness
10 awareness

48 Look, say cover, write, check

As usual, a visual strategy will reinforce learning.

INTERNATIONAL OVERVIEW

ANSWERS

1 football, basketball and bowls, in that order
2 bullfighting, then motor racing
3 table tennis, then (surprisingly) weightlifting

Diet and fitness

49 Pre-reading discussion

Students consider a new topic by looking at the role of food in getting us fit for a healthy life.

50 Predicting content

The pre-reading tasks, as always, encourage students to use textual clues etc to predict the content of the text, the target audience and the writer's intention.

51 Vocabulary check

ANSWERS

nibbles: snack foods like crisps and nuts, to accompany drinks
nibbled: ate in small bites
snack on: eat between meals
packed lunches: cold food like sandwiches prepared at home to take to work or school
sluggish: lacking in energy

52 Reading

The reading pointers will help guide students through Sheila's story. You could check them through afterwards and ask students to identify examples of the points in the text.

It will be interesting to see how students react to the story of someone losing a large amount of weight (four stones = 25.4 kilos). Let them discuss the topic freely. It's worth bearing in mind that the article's cosy style is in fact a marketing ploy. The magazine in which the article appeared hopes to persuade readers to use the Rosemary Conley approach to diet and fitness.

53 Post-reading discussion

The dieting industry and the media have been accused of promoting unreal body images. Students are asked to analyse the negative consequences of dieting. Hearing their ideas on healthy eating and 'the perfect body' should be fascinating.

54 Writing a summary

There are no comprehension questions after the passage. This reflects the way the exam summary

question is set. However, you may want to check that students have grasped the main points they should include in the summary.

MODEL ANSWER

The summary should read something like this:

Before Sheila lost weight she felt depressed about gaining weight but did not face the problem. She enjoyed cooking for her family and entertaining at home. The house was always stocked with tempting food. At work she ate food the patients gave her or other snacks. After work she would feel exhausted and take no exercise. Since she lost weight she has more self-respect, more energy and more enthusiasm for life. She finds the dieting plan suits her because she and her family can still eat things they enjoy, and she enjoys the fitness classes. *(95 words)*

You may wish to copy and circulate the model answer for students to compare with their own versions.

55 Vocabulary: Phrasal verbs

ANSWERS

1 start up
2 plunge in
3 give up
4 plucked up
5 conjure up
6 made up

WIDER PRACTICE

1 Summarising is hard, but remind students it gets better with practice! You could help them develop their ability to summarise by asking them to choose topics they have a strong interest in: interesting TV programmes, radio broadcasts, live talks they attend, as well as extracts from the written word. Their summaries could be presented to the class orally.

2 You could develop the sport theme further by asking students to research a sports personality of their choice and present a profile. Or they could research a topical issue in sport and fitness, e.g. sport sponsorship, women in sport, sports injuries, how to get fit for sport, weight control.

Students may be interested in doing a project on the history of a particular sport.

3 Students might enjoy visiting their local sports centre or swimming pool and finding out about its day-to-day operations, its role in the community, the facilities it offers, etc.

4 As students build up their knowledge about language, you could ask them to research an aspect of their first language or English and present an interesting talk on the topic. Fascinating possibilities include: the history of language, dialects, slang, loan words, affixes.

Transport Issues

OVERVIEW

This unit links the theme of transport to safety and environmental concerns, which are all popular IGCSE exam topics.

The main aim of the unit is to help students produce a 'for and against' article/letter for the school magazine or local newspaper. The exam is looking for the ability to present a convincing argument. Students are usually given a stimulus, e.g. 'A new airport is planned for your area. Is this a good idea? What do you think?' They can choose either to agree with the proposal, be against it or be even-handed. They are not asked to be 'for' or 'against' in a very rigid way.

The most important thing in students' answers is coherence. They should be able to develop the theme clearly, structure their ideas soundly and offer some exemplification and explanation. Candidates need to present the argument in a fairly formal style and have some sense of audience.

The reading items include a factual article on the steps taken to make flying as safe as possible, and a leaflet advertising a sponsored cycle ride to raise funds for the environment.

For listening development, students listen for specific information to a discussion on the results of a school survey carried out to determine the patterns of car usage among school pupils.

The discussion areas, as always, focus on encouraging students to think of relevant ideas and express opinions. This is even more important in an argument essay, as students can't produce a convincing argument if they can't think of ideas in the first place! Unsatisfactory compositions in the exam are usually very 'thin' in terms of students' own ideas.

LANGUAGE WORK

The language work focuses on developing reasoning skills. Students extend their understanding of the functions of linking words. Logical sequencing skills are also extended.

Spelling and pronunciation are developed by highlighting the contrast between hard and soft *g* sounds. Vocabulary development focuses on ways of walking, euphemisms and words often confused.

Fear of flying

1 Pre-reading discussion

The discussion focuses students' thoughts on transport and safety and asks them to consider visual data on accidents by mode of transport in Britain. As always, it's useful to ask them to relate this information to their own experiences. The discussion develops familiarity with interpreting visual data and gets students quickly into the topic.

2 Making notes

The safety of aircraft is a fascinating subject for discussion and students should enjoy studying the drawing, which shows the most significant aircraft safety features. The note-taking exercise lends itself well to some friendly pairwork. The information supplied with the picture is fairly dense and of a wide variety, so you'll probably want to check vocabulary items which might be unfamiliar first (e.g. *fire extinguisher, black box*).

ANSWERS

a before every (flight)
b (take place every) five years; (involve) entire plane being stripped down

c in tail fin
d in galley and near toilets
e Stand-by radios
f unpressurised compartment beneath passengers
g Fuel tank
h above seats
i Life jackets
j in passenger doors
k lightweight
l fire-resistant material
m Landing wheels
n Rudder can split into two

3 Vocabulary check

ANSWERS

1 *aviation*: the manufacture and operation of aircraft
2 *lifespan*: period of time something functions for or a person lives
3 *rigorously*: very strictly
4 *obsolete*: out of date

4 Reading with multiple choice

Students will have to read carefully in order to discriminate accurately in the multiple-choice exercise. Multiple choice is less common than other question types in the exam, but it is on the syllabus so it is worth practising it.

You might like to let students read the article once through as a whole-class exercise for general understanding, pausing in places to ask some gist questions, and then let them read it silently to find the answers to the multiple-choice questions.

ANSWERS

1d **2**a **3**b **4**c **5**b

5 Post-reading task

1 Encourage students to speculate on the qualities needed by air crew.

POSSIBLE ANSWER

Air crew need the ability to be calm, confident and methodical and to cope in a crisis. Flight attendants need greater patience and tact in dealing with people as their job involves more fact-to-face contact with passengers.

You could also ask: *'Would you like to work for an airline? What kind of work most attracts you?'*

2 Students may refer to the text as well as thinking of ideas of their own.

POSSIBLE ANSWERS

Flying is one of the safest forms of travel.

Each type of aircraft is only allowed to fly a certain number of trips.

Older planes are very rigorously tested, in accordance with the Ageing Aircraft Programme.

6 Language study: Logical reasoning

Logical reasoning is important in formal written arguments. Interesting exam compositions are sometimes marred by inadequate reasoning techniques, which mean the examiner soon loses the thread of the candidate's argument.

ANSWERS

A The words expressing reasoning are *because* and *As a result*. *Because* could be replaced with *as*; *As a result* could be replaced with *Consequently*.

B *If ... then* is a conditional construction: one thing depends on another. 'Then' is often not explicitly stated. A comma is often used after the 'if' clause.

You could elicit other sentences with this structure, e.g. *If the company closes, (then) jobs will be lost. If you pass the exam, you can go to university.*

C The word *as* is an alternative to *because*.

7 Completing a text

This exercise enables students to transfer some of the linking devices and structures they have studied earlier to a text about the dangers of using electronic equipment on planes.

ANSWERS

because/as/since, In addition/furthermore/ Moreover, If, then

It would be interesting to round off this section on flying by asking students: *'In what way has the article changed your views on air travel?'*

8 Spelling and pronunciation: The letter *g*

The aim of this exercise is to increase students' awareness of spelling/pronunciation patterns. Note that *gu* pronounced /gw/ is a relatively unusual sound and is often linked with words of Spanish origin, e.g. *guacamole, guava*. *Fire extinguisher* is the only example in the text.

RECOGNITION: ANSWERS

1s **2**g **3**s **4**g **5**s **6**g **7**s **8**s **9**g **10**s
11g **12**s

TAPESCRIPT

As in the Student's Book.

Other examples in the text you may like to elicit are:

forget (*line 4*), grounded (*line 54*), Chicago (*line 56*), regularly (*line 72*), programme (*line 75*), bigger (*line 162*)
and page (*line 1*), judged (*line 44*), engine (*line 56*), technology (*line 69*), obliged (*line 81*), managers (*line 134*), generate (*line 152*).

PRACTICE

You could ask students to contrast these sounds with voiceless sounds in English such as /s/ and /p/, where they can feel there is no vibration in the vocal chords. You might like to ask them to say *sssss* and let it gradually become *zzzz* (a voiced sound).

It would be interesting to contrast voiced and voiceless sounds in English with sounds in students' own language(s), to compare those which are voiced and those which are not.

9 Spelling patterns

This exercise builds on auditory discrimination by using a visual strategy to help students remember the spelling pattern in soft *g* words. Students scan the word list they have just practised and circle the significant spelling features. The soft *g* rule is a fairly trustworthy spelling rule, so it is worth teaching.

Remembering the spelling pattern for soft *g* words will help students spell a wider variety of words and provide some tools for decoding pronunciation. You could follow up this exercise by asking them to make intelligent guesses as to the pronunciation of more unusual words you write on the board, e.g. *pageant, ginger, gibberish, Egyptian, geography*.

10 Vocabulary

This exercise checks the meaning of words students met in the earlier exercise. Physically writing out the words will help retention of the spelling patterns.

ANSWERS

1 apology
2 oxygen
3 engineer
4 passengers
5 challenge
6 guarantee
7 regulations
8 figure
9 rigorously

Words 1–5 contain soft *g* sounds; 6–9 contain hard *g* sounds.

11 Odd word out

This exercise introduces some extra common words containing hard and soft *g* sounds.

ANSWERS

A regard (it has a hard *g* sound)
B pigeon (it has a soft *g*)

12 Look, say, cover, write, check

You could ask students to identify the reasons why these words pose spelling difficulties, eliciting ideas such as: '*Privilege* is often misspelled with a *d*; *ou* is a difficult pattern; *ie* words are often misspelled; the *e* in the middle of *vegetable* is silent and is often left out.'

You could round off this section on spelling by getting students to compose some fun sentences containing as many of the target sounds as possible. They then dictate the sentences to each other, e.g. *Hygienic Egyptian giraffes eat ginger.*

What transport do you use?

13 Before you listen

The pre-listening discussion helps focus students' thoughts on the transport they use in their daily lives. You could encourage them to think about alternative methods of transport and ask: *'If you had a completely free choice of transport, what would you choose and why?'* Hearing what they say will provide interesting glimpses into their lives and outlook.

VOCABULARY CHECK: ANSWERS

Get a lift from someone is a common idiomatic phrase meaning to ask someone to drive you free of

charge in his/her car. You could contrast this with *take a taxi*, which has a different meaning.

Acid rain is rain that is polluted with chemicals and causes damage to rivers, ecological systems, etc.

Asthma is a common chest disease which causes breathing difficulties and has been linked to car fumes.

14 Listening for gist / 15 Listening and note-taking

 As always, allow students to listen first for general meaning and then for specific information. Many of the notes paraphrase what is said on the tape, rather than using the same words. This is typical of the exam, which aims to test genuine comprehension and avoids 'direct matching' activities.

ANSWERS

1 11-20
2 50 car trips a week
3 80%
4 **a** is on a bus route
5 **b** too inconvenient
6 too dangerous/not safe enough
7 **b** health concerns/effects on health
8 the family needs a new car/parents buy a new car

TAPESCRIPT

You are going to listen to a discussion between two friends, Paolo and Linda, on the results of a survey. The survey was carried out to determine patterns of car usage by pupils in their school. Listen to the discussion first for general meaning.

PAOLO: Anyway, we've got the results of the survey now.
LINDA: Right, well, I can note the main points that come up and then fill in the chart. The school magazine is the best place to publicise the findings, don't you think?
P: Yes. Erm, well, you know, it's interesting to see the extent of car usage. Usually pupils are making between 11 and 20 trips by car a week. Mostly they're, you know … it's what you'd expect, getting lifts from their parents. A small percentage, 5%, make over 50 car trips in a week. The results really aren't encouraging.
L: Gosh, 50 car trips a week! That *is* a lot, isn't it? They must have a good social life! And understanding parents who don't mind being a taxi service! What was the response like to the question about whether there was an alternative to the journeys they make by car?
P: Well, a whopping 80% said they would get a lift even if they didn't really have to. They could easily have walked to where they wanted to go, but it seems they prefer to get lifts from their mum or dad. I think often it's just laziness.
L: Yes, although having said that, I do think a lot of pupils at this school do seem to walk to school.
P: 40% said they walked to school regularly but then, well, 33% say they always come by car, which is not so good.

L: I wonder why, when the school is on a bus route and there's a train station only five minutes' walk away?

P: Erm, well, from the survey it seems that coming to school by bus or train is either too expensive, or too inconvenient. Their homes aren't near a bus stop or train station – it's just not available where they live.

L: What did that 33% who come by car say about coming to school under their own steam – walking or cycling, for instance?

P: A lot of them said their parents wouldn't allow them to walk or cycle because it's just not safe enough. The roads are really dangerous for cycling, and some pupils live over eight miles away, so walking to and from school would just take too long. You can't really expect them to undertake that kind of trek every day.

L: What about wanting a car when they leave school?

P: Well, that was pretty encouraging from the point of view of protecting the environment. A third of those who responded were against having their own car when they were adults. One of the main reasons they gave was concern over the environment. They're worried about car exhaust fumes contributing to acid rain and affecting the wildlife. And they're also worried about, well, the health issue in general. They think car fumes can cause asthma.

L: Well, it's good to know they're not all desperate to become car owners themselves. But what about all those kids constantly being driven around in their parents' cars?

P: Well, one thing was mentioned. When the family needs a new car, a lot of children said they discussed what kind of car would be best with their parents. Er, they said they tried to, you know, persuade their mum and dad to buy a small, fuel-efficient model because that's better for the environment.

16 Post-listening discussion

It will be interesting to hear students' views on whether car usage should be restricted. If your students live in areas which are congested and polluted, they may be more inclined to recommend formal controls on the use of cars, such as road tolls, fines for being the sole occupant of a car, and limits to using the car at certain times of the day. On the other hand, if they live in areas of low population and open spaces, they may see no need for restrictions at all.

17 Euphemisms

Asking students to offer examples of euphemisms in their first language(s) would be interesting and also a good way of checking that they have understood the concept.

MATCHING: ANSWERS

1H 2B 3E 4F 5G 6A 7D 8C

18 Rewriting a school report

This is quite a demanding rewriting exercise, as it involves reading between the lines, but it should be fun too. Students could work in pairs or threes to do the rewriting. Afterwards they could take turns reading out their versions and you could ask them *'Which is the most direct? What would be the effect on someone if you told them that to their face?'*

POSSIBLE ANSWERS

English: Christopher's handwriting is poor/bad/terrible.
Maths: Christopher must learn to concentrate on his maths.
Geography: Christopher will have to give up this subject.
French: Christopher has/is a bad influence on the other pupils.
History: Christopher has been regularly late this term.
P.E.: Christopher makes no effort with P.E.
Science: Christopher must learn to be careful with the laboratory equipment.

19 Vocabulary: Ways of walking

The English language has a wide variety of ways to describe walking. You could extend the exercise by eliciting sentences which are appropriate for other kinds of movement, e.g. *glide, float, skate, slide, crawl.*

ANSWERS
1C 2D 3E 4A 5F 6B

20 Asking for a favour

Many students should be familiar with the situation of being dependent on someone else's goodwill. You might like to ask a couple of students to read the dialogue aloud first to highlight the appropriate intonation patterns.

You could ask *'Does Joe sound tentative or does he sound demanding when he asks a favour? Which sound is more suitable for the situation?'* You could then chorus drill a tentative, hesitant-sounding request so all the students get a chance to practise.

Remind students that *Would you mind …* is followed by a gerund (*waiting/giving* etc). You could also ask them to identify the more formal/less formal expressions, e.g. *put you out/be a nuisance* are more colloquial than *not too inconvenient.*

After they have practised the conversations in pairs, you could offer more prompts, e.g. wanting to borrow money, needing help to carry a heavy load. Or you could ask students to develop conversations around situations of their own.

Nature under threat

This section develops the theme of transport and environmental issues by focusing on cycling.

21 Pre-reading discussion

This activity could be done effectively in small groups as an alternative to pairs. 'Brainstorming' in this way continues to be a vital activity, as this is one of the most reliable ways to gather together enough ideas for a topic, which can later be fed into composition writing.

Students sometimes say they don't like brainstorming because it gives less motivated pupils the chance to take a back seat and let other people do the work for them. You might think it worth raising this issue in class and making it clear that finding the 'points' for a set topic is a shared responsibility. You can spread the burden of brainstorming by naming selected students to be responsible for the feedback from their groups to the rest of the class. You can also name an individual before the start of the activity to act as 'teacher' and write up an amalgam of the points from all the groups on the board. If you choose different students each time, the load is shared more evenly.

Setting a time limit helps keep students on task and makes the activity more tightly structured.

Some further possible advantages of cycling are: It's enjoyable/good exercise/cheap/quiet (an environmental benefit).

Some further disadvantages: You are exposed to rain and cold/bicycles can easily be stolen/they can't easily be taken with you in a car or on a train/you can't carry much with you on a bike/you need to be fit to cycle/cycling is dangerous on busy roads, during bad weather and at night/it's tiring.

You might like to highlight the colloquialism *bike* for bicycle.

22 Predicting content

As always, encourage students to be 'detectives' and to try to pick up as many clues as possible from the pictures in the leaflet, e.g. the group riding together suggests it is an activity for the whole family, the pictures of attractive locations suggest the route will be scenic. (The places mentioned are in the south of England, near London. Windsor Castle is one of the homes of the British royal family.)

Before they plunge into reading, you may need to explain that Friends of the Earth is an environmental pressure group, which operates through a few paid workers and a large volunteer force. They mount campaigns to raise public awareness of environmental threats. Anyone who sympathises can join and work for them as a volunteer in their spare time. It would be interesting to hear from students about similar organisations in other cultures.

Explain that in a sponsored walk or cycle ride, a sponsor usually promises to give a certain amount of money for each mile/kilometre completed by the person he/she is sponsoring.

23 Reading for gist
ANSWERS

The three reasons the bike ride is being held are:

1 for enjoyment
2 to raise awareness of the threats to the environment of road-widening schemes (the M3, M4 and M25 are motorways near London)
3 to raise funds for FoE's long-term transport campaign

24 True/false comprehension

Encourage students to scan the text to 'spot' the answers. Exam questions are usually sequential, but students should take care to read any information given in captions or individual boxes, if it is provided, as well as in the main body of the text.

ANSWERS

1	false
2	false
3	true
4	false
5	false
6	true
7	true
8	false
9	true
10	false

25 Post-reading discussion

It will be interesting to hear students' experiences of doing something for charity.

As road building is a very sensitive topic in the UK (but not necessarily in all other countries) and it features as a topic for the next section, you might wish to round off the exercise with a question-and-answer session bout the problems of road building schemes.

You could ask '*Why are new roads a problem?*' eliciting/prompting:

Roads take up a lot of space. Britain is densely populated, and valuable countryside has to be destroyed to make way for new roads. Cars burn petrol which produces fumes. If directly breathed in, these fumes can damage people's lungs.

'*How did pressure groups such as Friends of the Earth get involved?*'

In Britain people are given the chance to object to proposed new roads. There is usually a planning inquiry. In practice, the inquiry has almost always decided in favour of a new road, so people lost faith in the system and found other ways to protest. Protests might include setting up camp in the path of the new road and refusing to move. As a result, the roads cost more to build and sometimes the project is abandoned. People have joined Friends of the Earth (and similar organisations) because they mount organised campaigns to raise public awareness about road building.

'*What are the alternatives to new roads?*'

Many people argue that we need better public transport and better traffic management schemes, not more new roads.

26 Re-ordering an article

Students could work together in pairs or small groups to put the sentences into a logical sequence. Encourage students to copy out the article when they have finished, to reinforce their understanding of textual flow.

MODEL ANSWER

The suggested sequence is: f, e, l, b, c; d, g, a, k; i, j, h, with new paragraphs at d and i.

Audience awareness is important when students present an argument. It's worth asking '*How do we know the article is for a school magazine?*' In an article written for the general public, the 'you' would be replaced with something more formal and explicit like 'it frees young people from dependence on their parents'.

You could remind students that pronouns like *we/our* can be used to imply a set of shared values and assumptions between writer and audience. You could present a sentence like this:

We deserve special consideration from our families when we're in the middle of our IGCSE exams

and ask '*Who does the writer think will read this article? Who is he/she writing for – old people, small children, sportsmen, or students of the writer's age and background?*'

27 What makes a good argument essay?

The aim of this exercise is to get students to reflect on what makes a good composition: it should flow and it should be easy to follow; it should also be persuasive. The text they have just studied is even-handed because it gives similar weight to both sides of the issues. It's worth reminding students to give attention to the final paragraph of their compositions. It's a shame if the last paragraph of a good composition tails off disappointingly. This can have a marked effect on the grade given.

28 Presenting contrasting ideas in the same paragraph

An alternative style to that of 'The Pros and Cons of Cycling' is to present the contrasting ideas in the same paragraph, or even in the same sentence. This exercise provides a starting point into this style.

ANSWERS

Although I recognise … cycling, in my opinion it is essential …

I recognise … cycling. In my opinion, however, it is essential …

I recognise … cycling, but/yet in my opinion it is essential …

In spite of the fact that I recognise … cycling, in my opinion it is essential …

29 Presenting more contrasting ideas

Encourage students to work in pairs to complete the sentences in a logical way. Why not ask them to compare their answers with the rest of the group?

30 Language study: Linking words

There is a wide variety of expressions of similar meaning which carry out the functions listed in the headings. Students will certainly be aware of some of them, and the aim of this exercise is to extend their knowledge by introducing a wider variety of linking words.

POSSIBLE ANSWERS

LISTING: First of all, Secondly, Thirdly, In the first place, Lastly, Finally, Last but not least

ADDITION: also, moreover, furthermore, as well as, added to that, and, in addition

CONTRAST: but, however, on the other hand, although, even though, whilst, despite/in spite of (the fact that)

REASONING: because, as, since, for this reason

OPINION: In my view, To my mind, I feel, I believe, As far as I am concerned

EMPHASIS: above all, surely, in particular, especially, particularly, undoubtedly, there is no doubt

CONSEQUENCE: so, consequently, as a result, therefore

SUMMING UP: On balance, To sum up, In conclusion

Other headings to elicit are:

EXAMPLE: for example, for instance, such as, like

CLARIFYING: that is to say, in other words, namely

31 Brainstorming / 32 Text completion

The text completion exercise focuses on the environmental benefits of trees. You may like to ask students to look up information about the functions of trees in a reference book. Alternatively, they may well have discussed topics such as global warming in their science or environmental studies lessons. This topic gives them a good opportunity to explain what they already know.

Encourage them to think of some advantages and disadvantages of the proposal.

ANSWERS

1 Although
2 In the first place
3 also
4 Furthermore
5 because (*Delete preceding full stop in Student's Book.*)
6 yet (*Delete preceding full stop in Student's Book.*)
7 In addition
8 also

9 In my opinion
10 On the other hand

33 Discussion

The letter is appropriately formal. This is shown by the absence of colloquial language and by the formality of expressions such as *dismayed, improper, In the first place, Furthermore,* etc.

The writer shows an awareness of his audience by saying that he would be interested in what other readers think.

Roland's argument is convincing because he gives clear reasons for his views, e.g. the wood is a habitat for birds etc, the air is cleaner because of the trees, and a noisy, urban area is quieter. He also mentions the wood as a beautiful place in its own right.

34 Words often confused

The words in this exercise are regularly confused by IGCSE candidates.

ANSWERS

1	**a**	council
	b	counsel
2	**a**	effect
	b	affect
3	**a**	there, their
	b	they're
4	**a**	lose
	b	loose
5	**a**	alternate
	b	alternative
6	**a**	lightning
	b	lightening
7	**a**	practise
	b	practice
8	**a**	past, passed
	b	passed

INTERNATIONAL OVERVIEW

A The graph shows that the world's production of bicycles since 1950 has been consistently greater than of cars. Both increased equally steadily during the 1950s and 1960s. After 1970, car production levelled off at about 30 million per year, whereas bicycle production climbed dramatically to over 90 million – a ratio of about 3 bicycles to every car.

B The main reason so many more bicycles than cars are produced is probably cost. A car costs about 100 times as much. In addition to the initial purchase price, car owners have to pay much more for maintenance, as well as for fuel, tax, insurance and parking.

Cities and governments throughout the world have introduced various schemes to restrict car use (in addition to the well-known ones of parking meters and other restrictions). For example, certain traffic lanes in Seattle may only be used by vehicles in which at least two people are travelling; Britain is considering introducing peak-hour charges for private vehicles wishing to enter certain cities, in a bid to ease congestion.

A new motorway for Conway?

35 Pre-reading discussion

Use the pictures to focus students' thoughts and stimulate an interesting discussion on the advantages and disadvantages of motorways.

ADVANTAGES

They can be fast and efficient.

They link towns effectively, making business communications easier.

Building them provides jobs.

They reduce traffic on local minor roads.

They can be safer than narrow, winding roads.

DISADVANTAGES

They destroy countryside – need a lot of land.

They are expensive to build and maintain.

They pollute the atmosphere.

They are noisy.

They can encourage people to drive too fast.

Serious accidents can happen on a motorway.

Traffic jams can build up during road works or in the rush hour.

They can encourage car use, especially for long journeys.

36 Reading a model text

Students need to study the model text carefully. The style is suitable for a formally-presented letter to a newspaper.

37 Comprehension check

As usual, the comprehension check will make sure that even weaker students are in no doubt about the factual content of the letter.

ANSWERS

1 A newspaper.
2 Boost to business through improved communications; easier, faster and safer commuting; reduced pollution through tree planting; lorries will by-pass town centre.
3 It's convincing because there are specific reasons and examples given.

VOCABULARY: ANSWERS

a recession
b boost
c communications
d commuting
e nostalgic
f by-pass

38 Analysing the text

These questions focus on the overall structure of the letter and reinforce the linking words students have been learning. They might feel they are suffering from 'overkill' in terms of practice. If so, you might like to point out that the argument essay produces the least effective writing from exam candidates. Writing is sometimes list-like with little evidence of sound, coherent development. Writing in a mature, convincing style can be achieved, but they need to accept that a lot of practice will be necessary.

You may like to add a little more to earlier discussions about the importance of first and last paragraphs. Perhaps students feel they have no right to persuade someone one way or another, or perhaps they feel personally indifferent to the topic they have been asked to write about. Remind them that indifference (however innocently meant) will make a poor impression in the exam. A clear stance needs to be adopted, and a style and tone which sound persuasive will be well rewarded.

ANSWERS

1 *delighted, because*
  The opening paragraph grabs attention because it focuses immediately and clearly on the topic and uses emotive language such as *delighted*.
2 *above all* and *not only … also* are used for emphasis.
3 The opposing point of view is the concern over air pollution from the motorway. *On the contrary* is used to introduce a contrasting opinion.
4 *Finally* is used to show that the argument is being rounded off.
5 The last paragraph is firm and decisive because it uses emphatic expressions like *there is no doubt* and *really. If we want a bright future … children* is emotive and rather rhetorical

39 Putting forward an opposing viewpoint

In this exercise, students read an outline of a letter to the local newspaper which is in response to the letter from the Conway Business Group. As always, check that they understand the factual content of the letter before they move on to the next exercise.

40 Redrafting

MODEL ANSWER

Some sentences have been restructured for emphasis in this campaigning letter and to improve the flow, but don't worry if your students are unable to do this. The main aim is to add the linking words and paragraphs. Exclamation marks have been added for emphasis.

Dear Editor,

We were horrified to hear of the plans for a new motorway for Conway and we are sure our feelings are shared by many of your readers.

Firstly, we believe the scheme would destroy the environment and damage wildlife. Secondly, the motorway itself will cost a great deal of money to build. Using this money to improve the rail network will not only help local businesses but city commuters will benefit too.

The idea that the motorway will be more efficient is completely unfounded. The new road will soon attract heavy traffic and become heavily congested. Furthermore, the suggestion that planting trees alongside the motorway will help eliminate pollution is ludicrous. Trees can never make up for the destruction of wild flowers and wildlife!

Finally, many of us cycle or walk across the road to get to school or work. The new road will split the area into two, making this impossible.

Please, people of Conway, don't stand by and watch your environment being destroyed! Support the Conway Nature Society campaign by writing now to your local councillor.

Yours faithfully,

The Conway Nature Society

Students could, finally, read out their letters to the rest of the class and compare the efficacy of different linking words.

The Nature Society letter is, like the Business Group letter, one-sided. Both letters build up an argument in one direction only, so lots of linking words like *furthermore, moreover* are needed rather than several contrast expressions such as *however, on the other hand*. It would be useful to compare the effect of writing a one-sided argument with one that gives a more equal weight to both sides (such as 'The Pros and Cons of Cycling' on page 69). You could elicit the fact that a one-sided argument tends to be more emotive.

41 Relating to your target audience

This exercise consolidates earlier work on showing audience awareness in your writing. It provides some more examples of typical audience awareness statements. Once students understand the concept, they usually don't have too much difficulty with putting the idea into practice in actual writing of their own.

ANSWERS

A personal letter to a friend
B school magazine article for school pupils

C letter to a local newspaper for the general public

D letter to a magazine aimed at elderly people

E formal letter to an individual the writer has not met

42 Writing a letter from outline notes

This composition is quite stretching so allow adequate time. It might be a good one to set as homework.

MODEL ANSWER

A possible answer could go like this:

Dear Editor,

I play basketball in Antalya Place and I was very upeset to hear of plans to develop it into a garden for elderly people.

I know a flower garden would be attractive and brighten up a drab area. Also, the flowers and plants would be a habitat for a wide variety of insects. In addition, old people are often a bit lonely and they have no meeting place, so the garden would be pleasant for them to relax in. Furthermore, the trees would provide welcome shade, reduce pollution and noise levels and give some protection on windy days.

However, many young people live in flats and have nowhere else where they can play ball games. Also, our local teams won't be successful if they cannot practise, so team confidence will sink. At present we all use the area to meet our friends, enjoy picnics and watch matches. If we lose it we are going to be really disappointed. Boredom and resentment might set in!

Please everyone, don't take away our recreational area! We need it and maybe another arrangement could be made for old people so that they are happy too. I would love to know what your readers think.

Yours faithfully,

Miriam Court

43 Understanding a typical exam stimulus

Go through the prompts to make sure students understand each one. You could ask them to link the prompts to direct personal experiences they have had, e.g. Have they noticed litter being dropped by visitors near rivers they visit? Does it matter? Why/Why not? If there was a sudden influx of tourists wanting to fish in a local river, would it cause problems? Why/How?

44 Redrafting an exam answer

Using the exam prompts appropriately is a skill in itself. If a candidate answered in this way, he/she would probably receive a low D grade.

The positive points of the answer are that it is clear and easy to read, there are no language mistakes and the linking words are correct. Its weaknesses are that it is list-like, there is to much lifting from the prompts and little evidence of original thought. Trying to make the answer long enough by copying out all the prompts is a common error.

MODEL ANSWER

An answer which selects from the prompts and develops them could read as follows. It would be useful to highlight some of the key elements for students.

Should Our River be Developed for Boating?

Many of us have spent a tranquil afternoon lazing by the river that runs through our village. I'd like to consider the advantages and disadvantages of the proposed river development.

The river is in a lovely part of the countryside. People who live and work in the noisy, crowded city have a right to come and benefit from the peaceful atmosphere of the area. Moreover, if people come to the area they will spend money, which will give a boost to our local economy and many jobs will be created.

On the other hand, engine oil and litter from the boats will pollute the water. The blades from boats tear up plants which feed on pollution. This will eventually make the water dirty and stagnant. In addition, if too much fishing goes on, many species will die out. The sensitive ecology of our river will be ruined. It could just become a dump!

To sum up, I think it would be wrong to develop the river. Although we need to progress and become more modern, I think this can happen without sacrificing our wonderful river!

WIDER PRACTICE

1   Inviting a member of a nature conservation or pressure group to class to talk about their aims and projects could be a wonderfully inspiring experience for students, who sometimes feel overwhelmed by the thought of environmental problems. It's extra good if students can hear about a successful environmental campaign.

2   Watching a well-made nature documentary on TV or video can fascinate and enthuse students. It will lead to increased understanding of ecological issues, which can then be fed into classroom work.

3   There may be nothing to beat a day out to a forest or a lake to study nature in action. Nature Conservation Areas, Country Parks, National Parks and so on often have group leaders who are specially trained to teach school parties. They can supply wonderful hands-on learning about ecology, the history of trees, etc. A joint visit organised in conjunction with science and environmental teachers might be especially nice.

4   Getting and keeping informed of current topics in the news is no mean feat. Encourage your students to open their eyes and ears to what is around them. Their local environment may provide lots of stimulus for argument and discussion on matters as diverse as recycling, litter collection, whether women should work outside the home, or the value of rules at home and at school.

OVERVIEW

The main aim of this unit is to enable students to produce reviews of a film and a novel, orally and in writing, which are suitable for a student audience.

Reviewing appears deceptively simple. After all, most students watch films and many read for pleasure. Talking about films and books is a normal part of everyday conversation. Nevertheless, the skills involved in producing a concise, lucid and well-illustrated film or book review should not be underestimated. Films and novels carry us along with a flow of words and actions. There is a considerable challenge, even for native speakers, in stepping outside this imaginary world to formulate ideas and opinions on exactly what makes the film or book compelling.

The IGCSE examination rewards students who are able to select the key strengths, as they see them, of a novel, film, or live performance and explain, with reasons and examples, what makes the work effective. Both analytical skills and the use of appropriate language need to be demonstrated. However, the reviews do not need to be especially sophisticated, as the emphasis is on the ability to convey personal opinions thoughtfully and clearly.

THEME

The unit is thematically linked by discussions relating to the role of entertainment in our lives. Obviously 'entertainment' involves more than films and books. Try to encourage students to contribute information about any form of entertainment they have enjoyed. This makes the work more stimulating and prepares students better for the way in which the Oral Assessment is conducted. A discussion which starts with a review of a novel, for example, could easily progress to questions about the problems parents have encouraging their children to read.

The theme includes:

- what it feels like to perform or be otherwise involved in a work of entertainment

- the consequences of the trend towards home-based entertainment

- the effect of videos and TV on our time for and interest in reading for pleasure

- working in the film/animation industry.

UNIT ORGANISATION

The exercises are organised so that the first half of the unit (approximately) deals with films and leads up to an oral presentation about a film. The second half develops writing skills for book reviews. You'll need to bear in mind that students should gradually build on what they've learned as they progress through the unit from film to book reviewing.

LANGUAGE WORK

The language work focuses on strategies to help students analyse films and novels. These include developing awareness of important aspects such as characterisation, plot etc, and providing the means to discuss them. Specific language exercises include using adjectives and collocations, and the structures *so ... that* and *such ... that* to express personal responses to films. Spelling and pronunciation focus on the letters *c* and *ch*.

Talking about entertainment

1 Introduction and discussion

A This introductory exercise helps students to explore the role of entertainment in their lives. Encourage them to discuss how their preferences for music, for example, vary according to mood and circumstances, e.g. they may like loud music at parties but prefer gentle music while they are studying. Some students may want the escapism of TV soap operas or chat shows to help them unwind after a hard day, but at other times prefer serious documentaries or factual programmes.

B You could also discuss the special excitement generated by live entertainment. Students who have attended live performances could describe their reactions. If students have taken part in a live performance, allow them to describe the role they took, what they enjoyed about it and any problems that arose.

C Finally, ask students to say whether they would enjoy a job in the entertainment business. They could explain what personal experience, skills or qualities they think such a job would need and how these might be acquired.

The subsequent exercises are based on reviews of

films and novels. However, you could adapt them to include a review of live performances, including music concerts, poetry and drama evenings, live song and dance, and so on. Help students to understand that similar vocabulary and structures can be used to review the quality of the performance, the atmosphere, personal responses, costumes, musical and special effects, and so on. Candidates who do well in examinations have the ability to adapt their knowledge and experience to fit a particular question. This is very important in the IGCSE exam, which tests candidates by presenting new angles on familiar topics.

2 Film vocabulary

This exercise which checks film lexis would be ideal to set as homework to prepare students for the work of the unit. It's essential that they can use relevant vocabulary when describing a film. The exercise checks specialised nouns and a few verbs; subsequent vocabulary exercises will emphasise adjectives. You may like to point out that *genre* is of French origin.

ANSWERS

1 Oscar
2 performance
3 heroine
4 played by
5 role
6 plot
7 scene
8 cast
9 characters
10 directed by
11 box office
12 film
13 genre

3 Film quiz

Students should enjoy doing this film quiz, which aims to activate the often unconscious reasons for liking particular kinds of films. It ranges across personal feelings (favourite film stars, for instance) to more topical issues (should more films be made in your country?) It provides a starting point for thinking about what makes films enjoyable.

4 Pairwork: Asking for information

The paired conversation focuses on helpful phrases to ask for and follow up information. If your class is weak at the skills of discussion, why not drill the phrases before they begin the pairwork? More able students may need reminding of the value of actively incorporating these phrases into classroom talk.

After the pairwork, you may like to follow up any points on which students, depending on their background(s), culture(s) and previous experience etc, feel strongly. It may be simply a case of asking students to describe their favourite actors or the discussion may become more topical. For example,

they may feel that more films should be made locally or that there is too much crime shown in films today. It would be very interesting to find out why, and to stimulate debate.

5 Following a model discussion about films

 In this exercise, students read and listen to a conversation at the same time. The conversation is about the thriller 'The Hand that Rocks the Cradle' and the comedy adventure 'Crocodile Dundee'. The aim of the exercise is to show students the ways films can be analysed. They should follow the discussion in their books as they listen, as they are not really practising listening skills. If you prefer, they could read the dialogue aloud in class. The dialogue is constructed so that the aspects of films (character, plot etc) they need to use in reviewing films are shown as clearly as possible; unlike the taped exercises in other units, the dialogue is not aiming to reflect 'natural' discourse.

Before they listen, ask students if they have seen the films and, if so, elicit their responses to them. Otherwise, they can discuss what they think the films will be about. Ask students to focus, while they listen and read, on the teacher's questions and the way in which she follows up the students' responses.

TAPESCRIPT

See Student's Book page 192.

6 Aspects of films

Ask students to tick the aspects of the films that were mentioned by Sam and Carol. All the boxes should be ticked. To reinforce learning, you could go through the list and check that they understand how the vocabulary is actually used by the speakers, e.g.

'Did Carol mention genre when she spoke about 'The Hand that Rocks the Cradle'?'

'How did she describe it?'

'What other kinds of genre do you know (horror, westerns, etc)?'

'Did Sam talk about the hero of 'Crocodile Dundee'?'

'What did he say about him?'

Encourage students to find the answers in the dialogue in their books. The answers could be noted on the board, so they all have the same record.

You could round off the discussion by asking students which aspects of film reviewing would be useful for discussing a novel. (They all would be, except for the special effects aspect of films.)

7 Tenses

The plot of a film, play or book is usually described in the present tense. Carol and Sam describe their reactions to the film in the past tense because they are now looking back at how they felt at the time. In practice, native speakers often mix the tenses when they describe films or books. It is of no great importance, as long as the meaning is clear and there is consistency.

8 Comprehension

Although you may allow students to find the answers in their books, the question format is similar in style to those set in past listening papers.

ANSWERS

The following statements reflect Carol and Sam's views: b, e, f, h, i.

The reason why Sam and Carol convey the qualities of each film is because they give clear and exact reasons and examples. IGCSE students tend to generalise quite a lot in their answers, and the dialogue shows the importance of being analytical and succinct.

In Carol's opinion, evil can be shown on screen so long as the underlying message is that evil is overcome by good. This is a controversial view. You may like to ask 'Does this view justify any kind of evil being shown on the screen? Where would you draw the line?'

9 Language study: So … that and such … that

This structural review exercise practises ways of expressing personal responses. Expressing personal responses to a film (or book) is something many students find hard to do well. As an example, you may like to write on the board this sentence which is taken from a student's essay:

What with all the exciting music and sound of the guns, I thought I was inside the television.

Ask students how the sentence needs to be changed to become unambiguous, eliciting, for example:

The music and sound of the guns was so exciting that I was completely carried away/totally absorbed in what would happen next.

or

The film contained such exciting music and sounds from the guns that I felt as if/it made me feel as if it was really happening.

or

The exciting music and sound of the guns made me feel as if I was actually part of the action.

PRACTICE: ANSWERS

1 I was so keen to see the concert that I was …
2 She was so disappointed not to get the role of the princess that she …
3 The film took such a long time to make that the director …

4 It was such a fascinating story that the film company …

10 Involving your listener

Students should not have difficulty with the sentence completions. You may want to ask them to continue by originating some sentences of their own.

Recommendations and reviews

11 Discussion

The discussion aims to explore how technology is shaping our leisure time by providing more and more ways we can be entertained without leaving our armchairs.

The discussion is based on a Western way of life, where consumption of home videos, CD players etc is very high. If you don't feel that this is very appropriate for your students, you might like to focus more on the pleasures of going out to places of entertainment.

After students have completed the exercise, you could build up notes on the board eliciting their ideas. For instance,

ADVANTAGES

It can be cheaper.

It's safe, comfortable and secure at home.

You can watch a video several times over but only see a concert/film etc on one occasion.

DISADVANTAGES

Films are made for a wide screen and can be disappointing on a small screen.

Home entertainment feels less exciting than going out to a place of entertainment.

It's a more diluted, less concentrated experience.

DANGERS

Theatre and cinema audiences are declining in some countries, which may result in a shrinkage of the industries.

Places of entertainment close down, which can make town centres seem 'dead'.

The dangers of city centres etc become exaggerated as people have less experience of going out, particularly at night.

People become overweight and unfit as their leisure activities become more sedentary.

12 Choosing a home video / 13 A wider vocabulary

Using adjectives effectively is particularly important in reviewing. It is one of the main ways in which ideas in the film and opinions of it are conveyed. Vivid and revealing descriptions can transform mediocre IGCSE reviews into reviews which make a striking impression.

The dialogue at the video shop raises questions about habitual ways of talking about films ('that was good') which fail, in fact, to reveal much about them. Before students read the dialogue, you may like to write *The film was good* on the board. Elicit from students adjectives which convey information more vividly and precisely, e.g. *compelling, enthralling, intriguing*.

Students should enjoy reading the dialogue aloud, and substituting more effecting adjectives for *nice* and *good* in exercise 13.

14 Collocations

This exercise is quite tricky. You might like to encourage students to explore some of the more subtle aspects of collocation. For instance, a character is unlikely to be described as 'sparkling'. However, a character could be described as having a 'sparkling wit'.

If you share the students' first language, it may be helpful to make cross-cultural comparisons about which words can 'go with' other words. Or, in a multi-lingual class, you may like to encourage students who share a mother tongue, to make these comparisons in their language groups and produce examples for the rest of the class.

SUGGESTED ANSWERS

PLOT: impressive, magnificent, stunning, superb, enjoyable, satisfying, memorable, violent, bloodthirsty, amusing, hilarious, witty, sophisticated, quirky, sad, poignant, heart-rending, dramatic, gripping, breathtaking, mysterious, spine-chilling, atmospheric, intriguing, absorbing, thought-provoking, engaging, mesmerising, convincing

CHARACTERS: impressive, striking, memorable, tough, ruthless, embittered, revengeful, violent, bloodthirsty, amusing, hilarious, witty, sophisticated, stylish, quirky, sad, engaging, mesmerising, convincing, appealing, likeable, attractive

COSTUMES: impressive, striking, magnificent, stunning, superb, sumptuous, dazzling, glorious, memorable, hilarious, stylish, attractive

SETTING: impressive, striking, magnificent, stunning, superb, dazzling, glorious, memorable, dramatic, breathtaking, mysterious, spine-chilling, atmospheric, attractive

SPECIAL EFFECTS: impressive, striking, magnificent, stunning, superb, dazzling, glorious, enjoyable, skilful, memorable, amusing, hilarious, sophisticated, dramatic, gripping, mesmerising, convincing

PERFORMANCE: impressive, striking, magnificent, stunning, superb, dazzling, enjoyable, satisfying, skilful, memorable, amusing, hilarious, witty, sophisticated, stylish, sparkling, dramatic, gripping, breathtaking, spine-chilling, absorbing, thought-provoking, engaging, mesmerising, convincing

15 Understanding the style of short newspaper reviews

This exercise helps students analyse some of the techniques used by professional film critics, such as starting a review with the name of a star or ending with a question. The examples are of very short, highly-condensed newspaper reviews, which have almost a language of their own. Clearly, you'll want students to develop their own style, but they may like to adopt one or two of the techniques.

ANSWERS

A – B3 **C**2 **D**4 **E – F**6 **G**1 **H**5

16 Signalling information in reviews

This exercise shows the care that is taken by the critic in selecting words which are just right to describe a particular film. Students are given practice in identifying key words.

ANSWERS

1 adventurers, greedy, seeking
2 a **From** the snow-capped mountains … **to** a shark-infested water park …
   b pursues, attacked, assaulted, framed
   c rogue
   d is attacked, assaulted, framed, forced to defend himself (string of passive verbs)

You may like to explore the connotations of some of the words. For instance, *gang* in review A is used perjoratively, implying that the young men are thugs. Ask students if they can suggest possible alternatives and whether the meaning will change subtly. 'Group' would be a more neutral but less informative alternative. 'Annoyance' could replace *harassment* but it does not convey the sense of injustice implied by *harassment*.

17 Presenting a film to the class

This exercise consolidates the work so far by asking students to present a talk on a film to their group. Students should choose a film which they found memorable, if possible, as IGCSE students seem much more likely to do themselves justice when they are being enthusiastic than when they are describing boring or disappointing films.

Before students present their talks, it's a good idea to discuss the approach with them and to clear up any uncertainties.

ACTIVE LISTENING

Emphasise to students that the IGCSE oral assessment will be a positive, interactive process.

After a candidate has presented his/her initial ideas, the assessor will ask further questions on that topic and on related topics.

Encourage the student presenting the talk and those listening to take part in a lively follow-up discussion. Each student should contribute one positive response expressing praise or encouragement. You could practise the following beforehand:

Well done! That was a fascinating talk.

I thought that was very well thought out. I can see how much preparation you've put in.

Brilliant! I really hope I have the chance to see this film.

Students should also try to ask a question based on the talk, or a related topic, e.g. *Do you think there will be a follow-up or sequel? Do modern films contain too much violence and brutality? Do you think people are influenced by what they see in films?*

TAPING YOUR TALKS

If students tape their talks, encourage them to analyse the results in their groups. You may wish to select a strong example as a model for positive criticism from the whole class.

Working in the film industry

18 Pre-reading discussion

A The initial discussion gets students thinking about the film industry in general as an area of employment.

B The reading comprehension which follows is based on an interview with an animator who has become very successful. He has created a set of quirky, idiosyncratic characters and built interesting stories around them. They particularly appeal to young people.

Make sure students understand the concept. The photographs on page 85 will be useful. Elicit examples of animated films students have enjoyed. Ask them whether they found the ideas original and inventive, or childish and silly.

C Ask students '*What do you think would be difficult about producing an animated film using Plasticine models?*' Any of the following would be good answers:

making characters seem appealing

devising background sets

inventing plots

synchronising all the disparate elements of the action: speech to body language, interactions

between characters, movement of the items in the set.

D All the personal attributes on the list would be useful for an animator.

19 Vocabulary check

ANSWERS

eccentric: showing unusual behaviour
villain: a bad or evil person
Plasticine: a brand of modelling clay
models: small-scale versions
wire: thin string of metal that can be bent
phonetics: a system of symbols for representing the sounds of speech

20 Reading for gist

ANSWERS

Nick studied animation.

All the listed attributes are mentioned or suggested.

21 True/false comprehension

ANSWERS

1 true **2** false **3** true **4** false **5** false **6** false
7 false **8** false **9** false **10** false

22 Guessing meaning from context

ANSWERS

1 individual picture which is part of a film
2 people who gave him ideas or encouraged him
3 basic structure made of wire
4 in a real place
5 names of the people who were involved with a film
6 ability to notice and remember details
7 a job with regular hours, e.g. from 9 a.m. to 5 p.m.
8 extremely busy

23 Spelling and pronunciation: The letter **c**

The aim of this exercise is to raise students' awareness of how the letter *c* affects pronunciation. Wherever possible, vocabulary from the reading comprehension has been recycled.

Remind students that the rules for pronunciation help with spelling, e.g. words like *notice, peace, replace* keep the final *-e* when the suffix 'able' is added, in order to keep the *c* soft.

You may wish to discuss the role of character marks or accents, which denote how letters should be pronounced. Some words used in English from French, e.g. *façade,* are often written with a cedilla (although this is beginning to be dropped). Ask students if their language(s) use accents etc, and how much they help with pronunciation.

As always, encourage students to see that spelling rules are part of a larger language framework, not necessarily burdensome rules to be learned by rote. As students become more proficient at analysing patterns, their skills as linguists increase. This empowers them in other areas of language learning and enriches their appreciation, not only of English, but of their own and other languages.

PRACTICE: ANSWERS

/ k /	/ s /
Oscar	Wallace
career	scene
action	centimetre
comedy	Plasticine
discovered	advice
communication	certainly
accurately	influence
particular	recipe
credits	face
	cine

/ ks /	/ ʃ /
eccentric	efficient
accident	delicious
	sufficient

TAPESCRIPT

As in Student's Book.

As always, make sure students understand the meanings of the words, hear an accurate model, and practise saying them aloud.

Other words illustrating these sounds are: *identical, café, pronunciation, incident, spacious, gracious.*

24 Using words in context

This exercise provides an opportunity to practise contextualising the sounds. Swapping sentences and reading them aloud provides further practice. Encourage students to monitor each other's pronunciation.

25 Spelling and pronunciation: The letters *ch*

If you feel that students will start to feel overloaded by studying another pronunciation point, you could always come back to this exercise later.

Students will certainly be aware of the commonest contrast of *ch* sounds: / k / and / tʃ / . They are also reminded of *ch* pronounced /ʃ/.

ODD WORD OUT: ANSWERS

Group A: chef (belongs to C)
Group B: scheme (belongs to A)
Group C: chocolate (belongs to B)

TAPESCRIPT

As in Student's Book.

You could follow up this exercise by getting students to write the words in context or by giving them a quiz. In the quiz, you could test their

acquisition of the sounds by writing up the phonetic symbols on the board, with an example word under each symbol. Label the symbols 1, 2 and 3. Call out a word and ask students to say whether it belongs to 1, 2 or 3.

26 More practice of *c* and *ch* sounds

The discussion about a drama club production is an opportunity to practise the sounds in a reasonably natural dialogue. As always, encourage students to work in pairs and check each other's pronunciation.

27 Look, say, cover, write, check

Students continue with the visual strategy to reinforce recall of words which are difficult to spell.

Reading for pleasure

28 Pre-listening discussion

This pre-listening task asks students to think about what reading for pleasure offers. You may like to ask a student to build up the notes on the board, e.g.

You have time to absorb the ideas and can re-read sections.

It's intellectually stimulating.

It can make routine things more enjoyable (e.g. you can read on the daily journey to school or work).

Getting to know individual authors is rewarding.

29 Listening for gist

 Students are going to listen to a discussion in which a librarian expresses his fears that TV and videos are depriving children and young people of the opportunity to form positive reading habits, thus harming their intellectual and creative development. It's a controversial view, rather extremely expressed, for which there is no conclusive evidence.

A Jonathan's key point is that reading develops the mind, whereas videos offer quick, easy, shallow entertainment.

B The phrases the interviewer uses are: *If I could just butt in here … , Hang on!,* and *If I could get a word in here.* You may like to ask students how much success the interviewer has with interrupting. He doesn't succeed, even when the speaker has come to the end of a sentence, because the speaker is so determined not to be interrupted.

You could point out that *'Hang on!'* shows the interviewer's attitude – that he thinks the speaker is exaggerating. Elicit students' own personal strategies for interrupting, asking which strategies they would feel comfortable with.

TAPESCRIPT

You are going to listen to a radio interview. Jonathan, a librarian, is concerned that young people are giving up reading because of television and videos. Listen first for the general meaning and try to decide why Jonathan thinks videos are intellectually less stimulating than reading.

INTERVIEWER: What exactly are your concerns, Jonathan?

JONATHAN: I think it's very sad to see reading for pleasure decline in children and young people. Reading is a wonderful way to use leisure time. You can escape into an imaginary world of your own. Do you realise the average child watches 20 to 30 hours of TV a week?! Children and young people are not forming the habit of settling down quietly with a book, and getting, you know, the rewards of concentrating on a really absorbing story.

I: Well, if I could just butt in here, …

J: Children from poor homes watch most TV, maybe because their parents can't afford to pay for other diversions. However, borrowing books from the library costs nothing at all.

I: But surely a high quality film can stimulate young people intellectually and creatively?

J: A video, however well made, can't develop the mind in the way reading can. Reading teaches you to discriminate between good and bad in subtle ways. Most videos are about quick and easy entertainment, just as quickly forgotten.

I: Oh, now, I think that's a bit unfair! Where's the evidence?

J: Most videos and TV programmes are pathetic! The characters are shallow, the plots predictable. They rely on shock tactics to get attention – violence, aggression, crime, and abuse –

I: Oh, hang on!

J: … just to keep us watching. If crime is a theme in a novel, on the other hand, a child can think it through properly and come to understand the motives behind the actions of the characters. But I think violence on the screen is different. Children aren't using their minds to discriminate about what they see – they're just soaking up violent images!

I: So you're saying violence is more harmful on screen than when it's written about in a respected novel?

J: I think children who watch a lot of violence in films and on television come to accept violence and aggression around them as just a normal fact of life.

I: So you believe films and television actually influence behaviour?

J: Why would advertisers spend millions advertising products on TV if they didn't believe it was money well spent?

I: So, how would you encourage children to switch off the TV and open a good book?

J: Parents should set a good example by reading themselves. Our library has a special young people's section with some wonderful books! Parents can encourage children to join. At the moment, they're taking the easy way out and letting their children become telly addicts! Parents …

I: If I could get a word in here …

J: … parents should talk to their kids about what they're reading. They … they ought to ask their opinions of the plot and the characters. In the end, families would be closer too.

I: I don't think you should be too hard on parents! But what you say about screen violence and so on having a more harmful effect is interesting, though I doubt whether you'll be able to prove it! I wonder what our listeners think?

30 Detailed listening

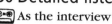 As the interview is quite a dense, complex passage, you may want to pause the tape in various places to check understanding.

The TV viewing figures are based on recent UK research. After the listening, you might like to ask students what they think the average number of viewing hours is in their own country.

ANSWERS

1 The habit of reading and the rewards of concentrating on an interesting story.
2 Reading uses intellectual powers which help you learn to discriminate between good and bad.
3 They come to accept violence as a normal part of life.
4 They can encourage their children to borrow suitable books from the library, and they can talk to them about what they read, asking their opinions of the books.

31 Post-listening discussion

Encourage students to support their arguments with reasons and examples.

32 Dialogue: Interrupting each other

Make sure students understand that the device **…** shows one speaker in mid-flow when someone interrupts.

Obviously, students will interrupt each other more than is normal in real life, but they will get valuable practice. If they have volunteered interrupting strategies of their own, they could also use them here. The views of the two speakers are deliberately rather black and white, as this makes their frequent interruptions more natural.

The pairwork adds more useful fuel to previous discussions about the influence of TV, films and books. Some follow up questions to ask could be:

'Can violence on TV undermine the moral values children learn in a good home?'

'Could examples of kindness and generosity on TV or in books compensate children who are being brought up in a harsh, uncaring environment?'

'If children were not watching TV, would they necessarily be doing something more challenging?'

'How useful is TV as an educational tool, teaching children to understand concepts or supporting the curriculum?'

INTERNATIONAL OVERVIEW

ANSWERS

A Library book loans per year:

UK (565 million)
Ukraine (520 million)
Germany (325 million)
Japan (203 million)
China (181 million)

B Most translated authors (*in 1990*):

Lenin
Agatha Christie
Walt Disney productions
N.B. The world's most translated book is the Bible.

C Most cinema attendances per head per year:

China (14.3)
Ex-Soviet Union (11.2)
Hong Kong (10.2)

D Most films produced per year:

India

(Statistics taken from *The Economist Pocket World in Figures* and *The Guinness Book of Movie Facts and Figures.*)

Writing reviews

33 Pre-reading tasks

A To prepare students for writing reviews later in this section, they are asked here what attracts them when they choose books. It's handy to bring in a few paperbacks of different types. Ask students what they can predict about a novel from the picture on the cover, the title and finally, the publisher's blurb.

B/C Before students complete the notes for a review of a book they have enjoyed, you may wish to go through the points with them, reminding them of useful things they have learned from film reviewing, e.g. keeping description of the plot straightforward, concentrating mostly on setting the scene, using a vivid vocabulary.

34 Reading model reviews

This exercise contrasts two model reviews, of a novel and a film, which are suitable for a school magazine.

An interesting discussion could be stimulated by asking students whether novels adapt well to the screen. (Some people say it is wrong to compare the two, as they are completely different media.) You could ask them to discuss this statement:

'*A film director, making a film of a novel, can show a viewer at a glance a situation which took many pages of description to build up in the book.*'

You could ask if anything is lost when a book is filmed (subtlety of character development, introspective elements, comments on life and surroundings, opportunity to really absorb and think about what is happening, etc).

The first review is of *Great Expectations* (published in 1861), a classic English novel by Charles Dickens, one of Britain's best-known writers. It is a thought-provoking novel in which character development is a major strength. You may like to discuss with students what they know of 19th-century life.

By contrast the second review is of a modern film, *Jurassic Park*, in which characters are less important than the plot. Hopefully, some of the students will have seen it and will be able to describe the plot and give opinions before they read.

COMPREHENSION CHECK: ANSWERS

Great Expectations
1 Great Expectations, Charles Dickens
2 In the 19th century, in England
3 Because he helps an escaped prisoner.
4 He becomes more aware of his faults, and more compassionate.
5 Because when he becomes rich, Pip forgets about promises he made when he was poor.

Jurassic Park
1 By a scientist experimenting in his laboratory
2 Because he wants to create a theme park, and wants to see what people will think of his project.
3 Because you never know when another threatening dinosaur will appear on the screen.
4 Because he has interfered with genetics.
5 Because it is too frightening.

35 Analysing model reviews

Students are asked to analyse why the reviews are effective, and to underline useful language for use in reviews.

You might like to exploit some of the expressions in the model reviews further. For example, there are a number of expressions using *do* and *make*, verbs which are often confused, e.g. Pip breaks *promises he has made*, the scientist wants the dinosaur park to *make an impression*, the director *does his best to make sure*. Elicit from students other examples, such as: *do a good turn, do the right thing, do a favour, do good/harm, make (a) noise, make a mistake, make an attempt, make a donation.*

36 Useful language for book reviews

This exercise asks students to tick expressions which they would like to use in their own reviews. They should also indicate which would be suitable for reviewing films as well. Typical reviewing expressions have been chosen which encapsulate ideas IGCSE students have difficulty in expressing well.

37 Criticising a film or a book

Students are given a chance to consider more mixed comments on books and films, which express both negative and positive views.

38 Effective openings for book reviews

Students are asked to rank a number of openings from students' writing in order of effectiveness. C and E are the most concise, vivid and informative openings. The others demonstrate typical tendencies to be vague, to ramble and a lack of appropriate vocabulary.

Why not ask students to substitute expressions from exercise 36 such as *It's hard to put down, It's compelling,* for the rather unfocused comments such as 'I couldn't leave any single moment in the book without reading it'.

39 Writing an opening paragraph

Remind students of the ingredients of a good opening paragraph for a review: clarity, being concise and engaging interest immediately.

40 Writing a review of a thriller from prompts

The Kidnapping of Suzy Q is a novel aimed at the teenage market.

MODEL ANSWER

'The Kidnapping of Suzy Q' by Catherine Sefton is the most thought-provoking and atmospheric novel I have read. It is set in modern urban Britain and it tells the story through the eyes of the courageous heroine Suzy. One day she is making an ordinary trip to the supermarket to buy groceries when the supermarket is raided. In the confusion the bungling criminals kidnap Suzy as she is standing in the checkout queue.

The criminals keep Suzy in captivity. Suzy recounts her ordeal in graphic and painful detail. I was impressed by Suzy's courage, determination and refusal to panic or give up. Several incidents in the novel reveal Suzy's ability to cope when she is threatened by them.

The story made me think how ordinary life is dramatically changed by a fluke incident. It is also inspiring because it made me realise the inner strength ordinary people can have to cope with disaster.

The novel is skilfully written. Catherine Sefton's style is crisp and witty, and the characters are strong and convincing. The plot is intriguing and never predictable. If you like spine-chilling, tense novels, you'll find this hard to put down.

41 Writing a film review based on a dialogue

Some of the advantages and dangers of using the Internet are:

ADVANTAGES

Fast, easy access to vast amounts of information.

Easier for people to work at home, e.g. doing research.

Space-saving way of providing information – less need for reference books.

Faster, simpler communication by e-mail.

DISADVANTAGES

Loss of personal contact, increasing isolation.

Lack of censorship – children can access harmful and dangerous material.

'Browsing' or 'surfing' can be time-wasting and expensive.

Writing the review could be done by two students working together, checking and comparing each other's drafts.

WIDER PRACTICE

1   Why not study a short story in class and analyse it in terms of plot, theme, characters, language effects and the ideas it conveys?

2   You could watch a video of a popular film in class and analyse it afterwards. Ask students to write video reviews and compare them.

3   You could try to arrange a talk to the class by someone involved in TV, radio, the music business, film or creative writing. Failing that, you could record an interview with a writer, film director, musician etc from English-speaking TV or radio (if possible) and discuss the ideas it raises.

4   The class could make a visit to a place of entertainment and write about it afterwards.

5   Some museums and art galleries will arrange guided talks and tours for school groups.

6   You could read a short play in class and perhaps even act it out. Students may enjoy discussing all aspects of theatre: the casting, costumes, scenery, stage direction, lighting and so on.

If students watch the same sort of TV programmes, you could ask them to be 'casting directors' and choose actors and actresses from favourite soap operas and so on to take the parts in the play. This could lead to a very rewarding discussion about the suitability of actors (age, appearance, voice, acting skills, etc) for different parts.

7 Students could discuss how to turn a short story or novel into a film. They could discuss what they would include and what they would leave out, as well as the setting/background, special effects, the costumes they would choose and who they would cast in the various roles.

8 You could follow up some of the ideas in the unit for composition writing or oral assessment:

- The reasons why we should start a drama club/music group/theatre group at our school
- A review of a wonderful evening spent at the theatre/a music concert/a festival of dance
- How is technology shaping our leisure time?
- Are we influenced by what we see on TV?
- What are the advantages and disadvantages of our increasing use of computer technology?
- 'No one will be listening to the pop music of today in 200 years' time.'
- 'Drama, art and music are the most important subjects on the school timetable.'
- 'Nothing can match the excitement of a live performance.'

EXAMPLES OF LIKELY EXAM GRADING

Do you like spiders?

No matter what your answer is, the movie 'Arachnophobia' will reveal the chicken in you!

Imagine a loving family moving into a nice and quiet little town in California. The coffin of a man who died from a spider bite brought back to his town of origin and a deadly spider hidden in the coffin. The spider reproduces and in no time the entire town is infested and people die, one after the other.

This chilling horror straight from Stephen King's imagination will freak out more than one of you, believe me, I have experienced it!

You will see some of the greatest visual effects ever made and a handfull of some of the best actors of the moment. Horror movie fans, you will enjoy this movie, there is no doubt about it!

The strengths of this essay are its wonderful sense of audience, crisp style and appropriate use of vocabulary.

This sort of answer would receive a B. More analysis and explanation of one or two specific examples could lift it into the A category.

The film I have recently seen and enjoyed was called 'Anthony and Cleopatra'. It tells the long and famous love story between the great ancient queen of Egypt and her beloved Anthony. What I really like about this movie is that it emphaises how love takes a great part of everyone's life no matter if you're rich or poor.

The film was directed by a very famous director. And with the help of the decorations, the garnaments and the make-up, we were able to drift away into the past. I was taken about 3000 years ago. To witness the beautiful love between the two ancient greats and to also see the sad ending. Unfortunately their love was soon ended by the brutal death of anthony and the sorrowful suisite of Cliopatra. Run now and get it on video. You'll be really glad you saw it!

The strength of this essay is the ability to convey personal responses to the dramatic atmosphere of a tragic film. This type of answer would receive a C. More analysis, more reasons and examples, and more technical skill with the language could improve the grade.

Travel and the Outdoor Life

OVERVIEW

AIMS OF THE UNIT

One of the aims of this unit is to develop a more mature descriptive style. Although IGCSE students are competent in many of the basic descriptive techniques, they often lack the sophistication or ingenuity they need to attract the highest marks. Moreover, description alone is not enough. Students also need to be able to explain *why* what they are describing is enjoyable and would appeal to others.

THEME

Constructive use of leisure time is the main theme of the unit. Leisure is a popular exam topic, and the emphasis is usually on the educational aspects of leisure, e.g. what do you learn from this activity? In the unit, 'active leisure time' is considered in a broad context and stresses the value of new experiences. These include: activity holidays, spare-time activities, camping, foreign travel and tourism.

IGCSE students sometimes tend to treat ideas superficially. The exam is looking for evidence of more intellectual depth. The unit tackles this need by posing questions which help students to think of all aspects of a topic. For example, if students are presented with an attractive idea, such as going on a foreign holiday, they commonly have difficulty in thinking of its less obvious, perhaps less pleasing points.

Areas for discussion in the unit are:

- How does a brochure advertising an activity holiday achieve its effects?
- What are the possible drawbacks of holidays?
- How can you be a responsible tourist?
- Can students hoping for new experiences by doing 'voluntary work overseas' really make an important contribution to developing countries?
- What are the pros and cons of working for the leisure industry as a resort rep?

LANGUAGE WORK

Students extend their range of stylistic techniques by learning more about using comparisons, relative clauses, *-ing* forms and the role of imagery in descriptions. Vocabulary is developed in a variety of ways, with work on adjective suffixes, intensifiers, colloquial expressions and precision in the use of adjectives. It is assumed students will already have some familiarity with the language forms. The exercises reinforce and expand their knowledge.

Punctuation of direct speech is studied. Pronunciation focuses on words with shifting stress.

Holiday time

1 Holiday quiz

The lead-in exercise focuses students' thoughts on what they want from a holiday. To consolidate this exercise, it would be interesting to create a class survey chart of the most popular and least popular holiday activities.

(The photographs show: Giza, Egypt; punting on the River Cam, Cambridge, England; the beach in Acapulco, Mexico.)

2 Pre-reading discussion

Students should be intrigued by the pages from a holiday brochure, which is specifically aimed at young learners of English. The summer camp concept is a repackaging of the traditional EFL study holiday. Students at the camp do a few classroom-based lessons a day. They then continue practising their English as they try out a variety of fun-orientated outdoor activities. Native speakers of English also attend the camp.

Ask students *not* to read the brochure yet, as this would pre-empt the brainstorming exercise. Instead, encourage them to focus on describing the pictures.

BRAINSTORMING

Students are likely to find thinking of BAD points about the holiday particularly challenging. You may wish to use prompts, e.g.

'Do you think you would see enough of ordinary English life if you stayed at a summer camp?'

'Could young students find the experience overwhelming and perhaps feel homesick and unsure?'

Some additional good points to elicit:

Learning practical everyday English
Caring staff
Safe environment to learn new skills
Making new friends
Wide choice of activities
Discovering more about yourself
Becoming more responsible

Additional bad points:

Homesickness/feelings of insecurity
Possibly not enough emphasis on formal English
Probably very expensive
May not like the choice of sports etc on offer
Little opportunity to experience everyday life and
customs in England

3 Reading for gist

Before students read, write up a model sentence
containing both facts and opinions, e.g.

*The sensitive, energetic instructors are aged
between 18–25 and are qualified in first aid.*

Ask students to identify the factual and the opinion
phrases in the example. You could also ask *'How do
you know this phrase is a fact?'*, eliciting the
possible response:

*Age or qualifications can be proved to be true,
but personal qualities are a matter of perception.*

4 Comprehension: Scanning the text

The questions test scan-reading skills. Remind
students that, although the questions might look
straightforward, mistakes can be made, e.g. question
4 asks them to interpret numerical data. Point out
that numeracy is NEVER tested in the exam – only
reading comprehension and interpretation.

ANSWERS

1   Three lessons per day
2   English youngsters also go to Camp Beaumont
    centres.
3   Beaumont Activity Village, Norfolk
4   £298
5   Boarding schools

5 An eye-catching advert?

A   The target groups for the advert are children
and their parents who will be paying for the trip.
The advert aims to attract these groups by the
'identification technique': potential customers will
identify with the pictures of teenagers doing fun
things, and parents are reassured that the fun is
balanced by learning.

There is a variety of opinion language, e.g.
*just the right mix of learning and fun, Every
minute of the day is filled with fun, excitement
and activities galore.*

The language, photographs and lively layout suggest
fun, interest, stimulation, supervision and good
organisation.

B   There is some factual information in the boxes
accompanying the photographs, e.g. *All the
materials are supplied by us, Three daily lessons
…, After you complete the course you will be
awarded a Camp Beaumont Diploma.*

Detailed information about dates, venues and prices
is displayed in the 'Where To Go' box.

6 The best way to learn?

It should be interesting to explore with students
what learning English through another medium,
e.g. abseiling, can offer. It will raise their awareness
of how and why learning takes place.

Ask *'What kinds of language would be most likely
to be learned?'* Possible responses are: listening to
and following instructions/explanations, language
to communicate to your instructor or partner that
you understand/need help/need clarification etc,
specialised vocabulary, conversational English to
discuss things with your partner.

7 Quite

The meaning of *quite* as a modifier depends on the
context, and, if spoken, on the intonation pattern. In
the brochure *'quite fluent'* means 'moderately
fluent' to provide a contrast with *'absolute
beginner'*.

8 Shifting stress

You may wish to give further examples, e.g.

There will be an *'increase* in prices.

Try to *in'crease* the amount of time you spend on
your homework.

(Similarly, *'subject/sub'ject*, *'reject/re'ject*,
'convict/con'vict.)

Elicit the fact that, in the examples, the stress falls
on the first syllable of the nouns and on the second
syllable of the verbs.

MARKING THE STRESS: ANSWERS

1   'produce
2   pro'duce
3   re'cord
4   'record
5   ob'ject
6   'object
7   'contrast
8   con'trast
9   'permit
10 per'mit
11 'present
12 pre'sent

TAPESCRIPT

As in the Student's Book.

Monitor students' pronunciation of the example
sentences, as it's important that they can show the
difference.

Many two-syllabled words change their function from noun to verb, of course, without a shift in stress. You may wish to end by eliciting some examples of these, e.g. *mistake*, *promise*, *display*.

Outdoor activities

The following sequence of exercises aims to help students describe free-time activities by highlighting useful language structures and vocabulary. IGCSE candidates are often asked to analyse *why* an activity they like would interest other people too. Here they are offered ideas of things to say and ways of phrasing them, and are thus armed with some techniques for writing in the more mature style the exam is looking for.

9 Pairwork

If you have a class in which students know each other very well, they could be more motivated to do an exercise like this if one of them goes to the front of the class and answers questions. The student in the 'hot seat' feels good about being the centre of attention, while the others enjoy observing how well he/she copes with a relatively stressful situation.

10 Reading: Identifying free-time activities

Suggest students read the descriptions in pairs so that they can discuss with each other what they think each activity is. Encourage them to find as many key words as possible.

ANSWERS

1 *Mountain biking* Key phrases: hard to keep the frame straight, muddy holes, pedal my way out of, descent, foot of the mountain.

2 *Jogging/running* Key phrases: without stopping once, good pair of trainers, slow down gradually.

3 *Archery* Key phrases: fit an arrow to the bow, pull the bowstring back, quiver, target. (Photograph: bottom left)

4 *Tennis* Key phrases: large outdoor court, hire a racquet, friendly games with a partner, concentrating on the ball, I usually get to most of the shots, perform the basic strokes.

5 *Riding* Key phrases: the saddle and bridle, mount by putting my left foot in the stirrup, trot, rise up and down. (Photograph: top)

6 *Swimming* Key phrases: submerging my face, artificial buoyancy aids, floating on my back, I feel as though I'm weightless. (Photograph: bottom right)

11 Writing in a more mature style

This exercise will make students more aware of the variety of ways they can describe an activity they enjoy. The contextualised examples (some of them taken from the texts in exercise 10) remind them of grammatical structures they will have met before, and show them how they can be used to particular purposes.

If students have difficulty with structures such as the -*ing* form, it would be a good idea for them to work on some specific grammar exercises. (Suitable grammar practice books are *Recycling Your English* by Clare West or *English Grammar in Use* by Raymond Murphy.)

If they have a reasonable grasp of the structures, a discussion of the examples in the exercise should be sufficient to refresh students' memories. Go into as much detail as you feel is appropriate. You could, for example, contrast the use of the infinitive with the -*ing* form:

We're allowed to use the school facilities.

We enjoy using the school facilities.

You could elicit further examples with *like, love, begin/start, intend, continue.*

Students can use 'since' clauses to make a comparison with their state of health etc before they began playing a sport or game and their state of health now, e.g.

I'm fitter/have stronger arms since I started swimming regularly.

I'm calmer/happier/more supple since I've been doing yoga.

Remind students of the way comparative structures are formed (adjective + -*er* or *more* + adjective).

Students can also study the use of similes, e.g. *If I can't go rock climbing I feel like a caged bird.*

12 Analysing language structures

Check with students that they have underlined the correct parts of the extracts. Actually going through the exercise might uncover gaps in their structural knowledge which you need to follow up with some formal grammar exercises – possibly for homework. It would be best to remedy problems before progressing to freer writing.

13 Describing a favourite activity

The consolidation exercise could be set either for homework, or as a classroom exercise if you have time.

If your students don't do much sport and prefer outdoor activities such as gardening, walking or photography, encourage them to write about these. The main aim is to achieve a clear, interesting description with enough detail.

14 Reading aloud

Students may well enjoy the chance to read aloud their description, suppressing the actual name of the activity and letting others guess what it is.

15 Pre-listening discussion

Ask students to study the camping picture and explore their responses to a camping trip, building on actual experiences some of them might have had.

You could ask:

'What challenges would living in a tent present?'

'What kind of clothes/equipment would you bring?'

'What might a typical day's camping be like?'

Stressful aspects of camping could include: coping with living in a small space without the amenities of home, the need to be super-organised, coping with storms or cold weather.

16 Listening for gist

 The listening exercise is based on a colloquial conversation between two boys relating their feelings about a camping trip. Asking students to listen for gist, will, as always, help them focus on the overall meaning of the extract.

ANSWERS

There are several things they didn't enjoy: the girls laughing at their attempt to put up the tent, the long walk in the rain, boots which leaked, missing the chance to see the museum, cold showers, no food for breakfast, cold showers.

Their intonation indicates that they enjoyed the trip overall.

TAPESCRIPT

Paul and Marcus have just come back from their first camping holiday with the youth club. What did they find difficult about the holiday? Note three things. Overall, do you think they enjoyed the trip, despite the difficulties?

PAUL: Do you remember that first night? I mean, we'd just arrived, couldn't wait to get unpacked and go for a swim.

MARCUS: And we couldn't get the tent up.

P: Well, that was my fault. I could have sworn I put the instruction leaflet in. I couldn't believe it when it wasn't in with the rest of my stuff!

M: Well, don't blame yourself. We managed it in the end.

P: I felt bad about it, though. That gang of girls didn't help. Remember how they were all giggling, watching us struggling with the tent half up?

M: Well, they got their tent up straightaway, didn't they?

P: Getting the tent up wasn't half as bad as that fifteen-mile walk in pouring rain.

M: And discovering that your brand new waterproof boots you'd spent 30 quid on weren't waterproof at all!

P: I blame the girls for that walk. We wanted to see the aircraft museum.

M: Yeah. It was their fault we got soaked and we never did get to the museum.

P: All because they were 'desperate to see a picturesque historic village with such a quaint-sounding name'.

M: Yeah, which turned out to be just like all the other villages around there.

P: Mr Barker always let them do what they wanted to do.

M: He didn't listen to what we wanted. Funny, wasn't he? With that woolly hat and specs. How old do you think he was? Fortyish?

P: More like fifty!

M: Remember when we had no food for breakfast?

P: Because the girls had forgotten to pack the food into airtight containers and everything was full of bugs.

M: Yeah, they tried to deny it, but it was definitely down to them. They were responsible for putting stuff away.

P: We had a good time, though, didn't we, despite the stone-cold showers ...

M: Rock-hard bread at breakfast ...

P: Trying to find the toilet in the pitch dark ...

M: Not being able to get any sleep ...

P: Because of Mr Barker's snoring ...

M: Getting up at the crack of dawn ...

P: Want to go again?

M: You bet!

17 True/false comprehension

ANSWERS

1 false
2 true
3 true
4 false (aircraft museum)
5 true
6 true
7 false
8 false
9 false
10 false

18 Post-listening discussion

The sort of things the boys might have enjoyed are: comradeship, independence, exploring a new area, making new friends, the challenges of camping, the countryside, physical exercise.

19 Blame

Students will probably need to listen again to the tape so they can really focus in on the expressions used.

ANSWERS

Students should tick all the 'Blaming' expressions, plus *It's my fault, I feel bad about it* and *Don't blame yourself*. (Note that in some cases the speaker used a different tense and/or pronoun.)

Blame and guilt are sensitive areas. British people tend to be indirect, so they are unlikely to say to someone's face 'It's your fault' or use the other phrases listed under BLAMING, unless they are angry. They do, however, use such language quite freely in talking about someone who is not there (as the boys do on the tape). Make sure that students understand the distinction.

Suitable expressions for blaming someone to their face are:

'I'm not really very happy about ...' (formal)

'I really don't know why you insisted on driving/bringing us here. Now look what's happened!' (informal)

Admitting guilt and absolving someone from blame are not sensitive areas, so the expressions listed can be used freely.

20 Comparing cultures

It will be enlightening to hear the language used in other cultures, and could lead to some amusing anecdotes!

21 Functional language: Writing a dialogue

Remind students to think quite carefully about the blame language they want to use. You may want to suggest that it's unlikely in the picnic situation that anyone would say 'It's your fault'. Perhaps suggest that students disagree over whose fault it is, each one being willing to take the blame, e.g. 'It's my fault', 'No, it was down to me', etc.

22 Colloquial expressions: Adjective collocations

In informal English, these noun + adjective and adjective + adjective expressions are common. You may like to ask students if they know any other of the numerous meanings of *pitch*. For example, it can be used as a verb in *to pitch a tent* and to mean 'a field' as in *cricket/football pitch*. This could be a good opportunity for some dictionary work.

ANSWERS

1 plain stupid (*plain daft/plain ignorant* are also common)
2 bored stiff (also *bored silly/bored to death*)
3 crystal clear (also used metaphorically, e.g. *his explanation was crystal clear*)
4 scared stiff (also *scared to death*)
5 freezing cold, wide open
6 sky blue (also *navy blue* – very common)
7 fast asleep
8 dirt cheap
9 wafer thin (also *paper thin*)
10 bone dry

Other examples you could elicit are: *wide awake, dead/dog tired, stone deaf, boiling/scorching hot, stone cold* (of food), *razor sharp, raving mad.*

23 More colloquial expressions

English is very rich in all kinds of colloquial expressions. Understanding their use and being able

to use them will make a terrific difference to students' fluency.

ANSWERS

1 a bite to eat
2 a drop of rain
3 hear a pin drop
4 a speck of dirt
5 a hair out of place
6 in the nick of time
7 a penny to his name
8 a stroke of work

Before students try to create their own expressions, remind them that they need to use the whole phrase. You could round off the exercise by asking them to share any similar colloquial expressions from their own language(s).

24 Word building: Adjective suffixes

Remind students that *e* and *y* are dropped from the end of words when adding a suffix beginning with a vowel.

ANSWERS

1 bulletproof
2 twentyish
3 ironic
4 odd-sounding, odd-looking
5 childish, childlike, childproof, childless
6 statuesque
7 Arabic
8 boyish
9 panoramic
10 soundproof
11 Islamic
12 pleasant-sounding, pleasant-looking
13 scenic
14 pinkish

Other examples you could elicit are: *foolproof, girlish, foreign-sounding, allergic, energetic, athletic, box-like, lady-like.*

You could also ask students what other adjective suffixes they are aware of, e.g.

-ical: *grammatical, theatrical, alphabetical*

-worthy: *seaworthy, roadworthy, trustworthy, newsworthy*

-some: *quarrelsome, tiresome, awesome, troublesome*

-ous: *poisonous, dangerous, courageous*

-ious: *ambitious, suspicious, infectious*

-ful: *helpful, delightful, meaningful, peaceful*

-y, -ly: *windy, spicy, friendly, ghostly*

-able, -ible: *memorable, fashionable, inedible*

25 Punctuating direct speech

Many IGCSE students can use inverted commas around the actual words used by a speaker, but they don't use other elements needed for direct speech like the commas or capital letters. This exercise aims to encourage students to work deductively, so allow them sufficient time to analyse the examples, prompting where necessary. The exercise also provides more descriptive language to add to students' growing repertoire.

Remind students that if you start a new paragraph when the speaker is in the middle of a speech, you don't need to close inverted commas at the end of the paragraph. They do need to be opened, however, at the beginning of the next paragraph.

PRACTICE: ANSWER

'What was the best part of your holiday in America?' Naomi asked when she saw Kevin again.

'Going along Highway One from Los Angeles to San Francisco,' said Kevin, without hesitation. 'I wouldn't have missed it for the world.'

'What's so special about Highway One?' Naomi asked, wrinkling her nose. 'Isn't it just another dead straight American highway?'

'Well,' replied Kevin. 'The road runs between … redwoods. Yes,' he paused for a moment, 'it's truly magnificent.'

'What was the weather like?' Naomi asked thoughtfully. 'Every time I checked the international weather forecast there was one word: hot.'

'In fact,' Kevin laughed, 'we had stormy weather, but when the sun broke through it created fantastic rainbows. We visited a jade cove where you can hunt for jade. Anything you find is yours and I'd almost given up looking when I found this.' He reached into his pocket and pulled out a tiny green fragment. 'Here,' he said, 'it's for you.'

Tourism: The pros and cons

26 Brainstorming

The IGCSE exam is looking for evidence of depth of thought. Awareness of topical issues and an ability to discuss them thoughtfully are always rewarded. This exercise is very challenging, and it's a good idea for students to do it in small groups before coming into a larger group to pool their ideas.

The following may give you some ideas of what students could produce.

PLEASURES OF BEING A TOURIST

Having new experiences - observe customs, sample local cuisine, visit local places of interest perhaps very different from home country.

Having more time to explore things/learn a skill/meet people.

You can practise the local language.

You go home with more understanding of a different part of the world.

If you want a suntan, you may get one.

DRAWBACKS OF BEING A TOURIST

You may be adversely affected by strange food, a different climate, different culture.

Lack of knowledge of the locality/language may cause frustrations/misunderstandings and you may even be exploited by unscrupulous people.

You may be homesick.

You may find the country you are visiting disappointing and very different from your expectations.

You may get sunburnt/bitten by insects/lost in a strange place or lose your valuables.

ADVANTAGES TO THE HOST COUNTRY

Tourism creates employment of various kinds - service industries, construction, manufacturing.

Earns foreign currency.

Tourism can create more international harmony.

The wealth generated by tourism can be invested in the economy to improve the infrastructure - roads, hospitals, schools, etc.

Some facilities built with tourists in mind may benefit the local population, e.g. wildlife parks, swimming pools, etc.

DISADVANTAGES TO THE HOST COUNTRY

The natural beauty of a locality may be destroyed by insensitive development.

People may be displaced to make way for tourist facilities, e.g. indigenous people moved off land to create safari parks.

The local economy may become distorted as plantations, rice paddies and pasture land used by farmers are destroyed to build golf courses, hotels, safari parks, etc.

Local fishermen may be denied access to beaches to work.

Wildlife may be negatively affected.

HOW CAN TOURISTS BEHAVE RESPONSIBLY WHEN THEY GO ABROAD?

Save precious natural resources and energy, e.g. they shouldn't waste water and should switch off lights.

Avoid buying items made from endangered species, e.g. ivory.

Ask (using gestures if necessary) before taking photos/videos of people.

Respect the local etiquette – dress modestly and avoid behaviour in public which may offend.

Learn about their host country's history and current affairs.

You may like to ask a student to write up the ideas from the whole class on a board or flip chart, if there is time.

(The photograph shows the temple of the Parthenon, Athens.)

27 Tourism with a difference

Ask students what they think of 'sustainable tourism', and elicit examples of ways it could be implemented in students' own countries.

28 Pre-reading discussion

The reading comprehension exercise which follows is from a magazine article encouraging British holidaymakers to visit two lovely Italian islands, Sicily and Sardinia.

Before they begin reading, it's interesting to hear students' perceptions of these islands, and also to find out how they think foreigners view students' own country(ies). You could link their answers to the results of the earlier discussion about tourism as a world-wide issue.

If students have travelled abroad, you could ask what their expectations of the country were before they went, and how the visit modified their perceptions.

29 Vocabulary check

ANSWERS

1H **2**E **3**A **4**F **5**J **6**D **7**G **8**B **9**I **10**C

Incandescently is an unusually long word. You could ask students to work out how many different words they can make from it by rearranging the letters.

30 Reading and underlining

Underlining the descriptive passages will reinforce awareness of description, one of the unit's main aims.

31 Comprehension check

ANSWERS

1 Their physical separation from the mainland.

2 Markets like souks and couscous cafés in the capital remind the writer of North Africa.

3 There are some of the most beautifully decorated buildings in that part of the world.

4 Any two of: fishing, cycling, walking, riding.

5 Any one of: wilderness, wildlife, prehistoric stone dwellings called 'nuraghi'.

32 Post-reading discussion

It's fascinating to explore the contradictory needs of tourists and the difficult position it places tour operators in, e.g. the wish to be immersed in an exotic culture but find familiar foods from home.

You could ask: '*How far should tour operators meet the needs of holidaymakers, e.g. wanting cups of tea in the wilderness, or hotel-levels of comfort when staying with local families on remote farms?*'

33 Adverbs as intensifiers

Intensifying adverbs are common in English. It's difficult to give hard and fast rules about their use, but you could tell students that adverbs like *appallingly*, *horrifyingly*, etc collocate with negative words. *Terribly*, however, collocates with positive as well as negative adjectives, e.g. *terribly good-looking*, *terribly nice* and *terribly difficult*, *terribly expensive*.

Adverbs like *staggeringly*, *amazingly*, *incredibly* are used when there is a suggestion of surprise, e.g. *The balcony had a staggeringly beautiful view of the bay.*

ANSWERS

1 appallingly/surprisingly
2 fully
3 strikingly/strangely/surprisingly
4 badly
5 seriously
6 utterly
7 dazzlingly/surprisingly
8 surprisingly
9 painstakingly/badly
10 faintly
11 alarmingly
12 strangely/surprisingly

34 Imagery in descriptions

The following sequence of exercises focuses on bringing together what students have learned so far about describing, building on the earlier work on describing a spare-time activity. Using a combination of techniques will produce a more mature style which will be well rewarded in the exam and a life-long asset to them.

Encourage students to draw on all their language resources in responding to the question on imagery. For example, a good response to *a lovely, broad landscape with rolling plains and corn-coloured hills* would be: 'When I hear this, I think of an open, peaceful and fertile landscape, with an unhurried, natural way of life.'

By contrast, the description of the starker landscape of Sardinia in *Eagles and black vultures soar over the mountains, pink flamingos flash their wings by the coast* might elicit the response: 'It suggests a wild, untamed atmosphere, lots of contrasts, very colourful, lots of fascinating things to see.'

35 Adjectives: Quality not quantity

Students continue to investigate the power of language by observing how many descriptive adjectives are used before a noun. It's usually only one or two, and the students can reflect on the tremendous effect that well-chosen adjectives have on creating atmosphere.

Encourage students to choose an example of descriptive language and explore it.

36 Comparing two styles

Comparing and contrasting the two styles will bring descriptive techniques into sharper focus for students. Style 1 reflects the way many IGCSE candidates write – in simple, short sentences, with a limited vocabulary, resulting in a repetitive, long-winded style. Students need to move on from this. Style 2 is more mature and integrates the techniques students have been learning so far: intensifiers, a broad vocabulary and more complex sentences.

37 Developing a mature style

PRACTICE

Students could work in pairs to draft and redraft the description. Remind them of the value of perseverance. A graceful, mature style takes time and effort to acquire in a first language, let alone a second language! Yet the skills they are acquiring will make an enormous difference not only to exam grades, but to their communicative ability in all kinds of contexts.

MODEL ANSWER

Students could produce something like this:

The town developed around an ancient rectangular marketplace. It has many medieval buildings and a wide diversity of restaurants offering delicious food from several different cultures. The local people have a traditional way of life and dress, and are very hospitable, honest and welcoming.

38 Writing your own description

This would be a good homework exercise. Encourage students to make as many drafts as they feel are necessary.

INTERNATIONAL OVERVIEW

Namibia receives about half the amount of money that South Africa receives.

If you have students who still have difficulty understanding tables, tell them to study the chart and ask more basic questions first about which countries receive the most/least income from tourism, before asking the question set in the Student's Book.

Why not encourage your students to find these countries on a map of Africa?

You could discuss the reasons tourists go to Africa (scenery, climate, interesting cultures, wildlife, safaris and so on). If you have African students, it would be good to give prominence to their views. You could also find out which countries in the world your students would most like to visit.

39 Giving a short talk

You may like to tape a few of the best talks for analysis later.

40 Words from names

Some verbs such as *pasteurise* (milk) or nouns such as *sandwich* are, of course, named after the individuals who invented them. In this exercise, students match the invention to the name of the person.

ANSWERS

1 Sandwich
2 Cardigan
3 Pasteur
4 Fahrenheit
5 Morse
6 Volta
7 Marx
8 Diesel

Encourage students to think of the alterations which are made to some of the names to turn them into verbs or adjectives: *Pasteur + -ise, Marx + -ist*.

Names, their meanings, origins and associations, are a source of great interest. Even if something is never named after us, names are tremendously important in our identity. We all like to know what our first name 'means'. In multi-cultural classrooms, there is a wonderful opportunity for students to share a great wealth of cultural knowledge about naming systems. Sometimes students have an adopted English name and are aware that the name of their country or city has a different name in English. Some people moving to settle in Britain anglicise their family names. Again, this is fascinating to discuss and to draw international comparisons.

The discussion could also stimulate exploration of how family and place names originated. Many English family names were derived from place names (*York, Worthington*), nicknames (*Armstrong*), family relationships (*Johnson*) and trade names (*Carpenter, Baker*).

Ask students to contribute what they know about the origins of names in their culture. This would be fascinating for everyone. It would be rewarding for students to investigate the meanings and origins of their own first and family names and to present a little talk to the class.

The impact of modern life on names could also be investigated, with students asked to reflect on trademark names such as *biro, hoover,* and *walkman*, which have slipped into the everyday language.

41 More homophones

This exercise gives further practice with homophones taken from the reading texts. Some are less obvious than others, e.g. *boar/bore*. This will give students more insight into the range of homophones in English.

ANSWERS

1 reel
2 bore
3 see
4 sore
5 to/too
6 heard
7 seen
8 flour
9 write/rite
10 blew
11 sale
12 dear

Personal challenges

42 Reading a model letter

As always, the model letter provides a reliable example of the sort of writing students should be aiming for.

43 Comprehension

ANSWERS

1 Wales
2 She was nervous/apprehensive. Her feelings *weren't* justified – she didn't feel lonely because the group leaders were so thoughtful.
3 Canoeing
4 It's stimulating, you feel independent, you get the chance to learn new skills and you learn in a safe environment.
5 She loved it and wants to do it again.

44 Analysing the letter

ANSWERS

1 Para 1: reason for writing
   Para 2: description of place and weather
   Para 3: description of canoeing lessons
   Para 4: why Lucia would enjoy it, too

2 This question highlights and revises the main language skills students have learned so far. They should try to comment on the use of adjectives, intensifiers and complex clauses.

3 Students sometimes find it difficult to say why something they like would also interest others. This paragraph gives another example of how to do this, with useful expressions for closing a letter.

45 Vocabulary: The weather

ANSWERS

1 false
2 false
3 true
4 true
5 false
6 true
7 true
8 true
9 true
10 false

46 Spelling revision

This exercise gives students the chance to revise some of the spelling rules they learned in earlier units (see pages 30/31 and 53).

47 Writing about the weather

ANSWER

We're having a good time here but the weather isn't great. Every day starts *misty* or even *foggy*. This clears up by midday and we get a little *hazy* sunshine. We had a *rainy* day yesterday and the ground was too *muddy* for walking. It's generally *chilly* and I'm glad we brought warm clothes. Our boat trip was cancelled because it was *stormy*. We're hoping for calmer weather tomorrow.

48 Discussion: Voluntary work abroad

Voluntary work overseas attracts many idealistic young people who want to help developing countries and get more life experiences. In the past it was sometimes claimed that the people who went on the schemes were too inexperienced and untrained to do anything much except feel homesick!

It will be fascinating to hear students' views, especially if they come from the less affluent countries. Elicit from them the ways of overcoming potential problems caused by inexperience which are in place in voluntary organisations, e.g. induction schemes, vocational training for the work students will do, acclimatisation periods, etc.

49 Building a letter from notes

The letter could be checked by getting students to complete it on the board.

ANSWER

The first month I was very lonely but now I am beginning/have begun to enjoy myself here. The climate is warm and sunny, except for last night when there was a big storm which turned (the) paths into rivers.

The family I am staying with are very kind. The house is three-bedroomed and is quite comfortable. I am very close to my 'sisters', who tell me off if I do anything wrong! Each morning I wake up to/am woken by the sound of exotic birds darting among the trees.

Yesterday, I took a bus through breathtaking countryside to the local city. I went to a bustling market. Everywhere people were selling things but I am/was not sure who was buying!

I am helping to teach young children in a junior school. The children are delightful and are very polite. The work is demanding but rewarding.

I miss everyone at home but I feel I am growing up/have grown up quickly and I am more confident now.

50 Look, say, cover, write, check

Students often enjoy regular short tests, as they get a sense of progress and achievement from them. As usual, in this exercise they learn problematic spellings.

51 Discussion: Working as a tour guide

You may like to check that students understand what a tour guide actually does before going into the activity in the Student's Book. They need to understand that tour guides are normally employed by a travel company to look after tourists who have booked holidays with the company. Their duties may include interpreting and explaining to tourists things they need to know about the places they are staying in, e.g. the opening times of shops, how to get a doctor. They will help sort out problems tourists encounter, such as getting ill or losing valuables on the trip. The job usually includes taking the group to places of interest and places of entertainment in the evening.

Depending on the type of trip, a guide may accompany the group to other cities or destinations on the itinerary, or even across continents. Tour guides usually wear some sort of uniform so they are easily recognisable. Point out that, unlike a tour guide, a resort rep (= representative) is usually based in one specific holiday resort.

52 Reordering a magazine article

ANSWER

The correct order is: l, j, e, m, c, d, n, f, a, h, k, b, g, i.

You may like to circulate a copy of the completed newsletter article.

First of all, let me give you an idea of what Rhodes is like. It's got an impressive old town and a new town with graceful, modern buildings. In addition, there are many stunning, unspoilt beaches and peaceful villages.

Next, I'd like to tell you a bit about my job. The work itself is very varied and I have the opportunity to meet new people and see interesting places. I have groups of all ages. At

the moment, for example, I'm looking after a group of elderly people. It is the first time they have been abroad. Initially, they relied a lot on me to explain about the banks and shops and to recommend local restaurants and the best sightseeing trips. Now, however, they are much more relaxed. In fact, they are more independent than many much younger tourists.

Finally, I hope this has given you some idea of what life as a resort rep is all about. Although it gives you the chance to have lots of fun, it's not all glamour. However, if any of you are keen to get involved, I would definitely recommend it!

Exam-format questions

Form-filling

In Paper 1, Part 2, exercise 3, Core candidates have to fill in a form. They are usually asked to read a scenario and complete the form as though they are the person in the scenario. Candidates sometimes have to fill in a form on behalf of other people, e.g. they might need to book a school party into a theatre/for a zoo visit.

The form is usually adapted from an authentic source and may be an application form, booking form, questionnaire, evaluation form, accident report form, mail order form, etc. It's a good idea to give students plenty of practice. The more able Core candidates could even design a form based on information you give them. For example, you could provide a scenario about an accident at school (e.g. cut hand on glass beaker in science lesson) and ask students to design questions for the accident report form.

Common exam mistakes are:

* filling in the form for themselves, not the person in the scenario

* mistakes in the detail, e.g. names, addresses and telephone numbers need to be error-free to receive the marks allocated. This is on the grounds that such information should be completely accurate if it is to communicate.

* not using block capitals when specified.

The **postcode**, if given as part of the address, may present difficulties because postcodes are not used by everybody and many candidates do not understand what they are. It's useful to go over what a postcode is and what a British postcode looks like, e.g. EH4 5JR, B15 9TT. If the form asks for 'Postcode' separately then it should be written on the appropriate line as a freestanding piece of information. Otherwise it should be put after the name of the town as part of the address. Leaving out the postcode is counted as an error.

Candidates need to understand the language of forms, e.g. *please specify*, *delete whichever is not applicable*, *please circle*, *block capitals only*.

Understanding of the situation in general is required, as students need to interpret information. The scenario often uses words and phrases of similar meaning to those found on the form, rather than exact matches.

The form usually asks for 12 bits of information, with half a mark for each, giving a final total of 6 marks for the exercise. Marks are rounded up to a whole number for the final total, if necessary. The form is the only exam exercise where half marks are awarded.

HOLIDAY EVALUATION FORM: ANSWERS AND MARKS

Name: Lin Ho *(half mark)*

Address: 12 Legaspi Towers, 200 Roxas Road, Metro, Manilla, Philippines *(half mark if all correct)*

Please circle your age group: (16-9) *(half mark)*

Length of stay: Seven days ☑ *(half mark)*

How did you reach the Park?:
By boat ☑ *(half mark)*

Accommodation:
Riverside accommodation ☑ *(half mark)*

The standard of accommodation was:
average ☑ *(half mark)*

What activities did you participate in:
Visiting caves ☑ *(half mark for*
Nature trails ☑ *3 correct*
Birdwatching ☑ *ticks)*

The guide was: generally helpful and
well informed ☑ *(half mark)*

Did you encounter any dangers on the trip?
Yes ☑ *(half mark)*

If *yes*, did the encounter require First Aid?
No ☑ *(half mark)*

What was the highlight of the trip in your opinion?
Seeing a cloud of bats at the Deer Cave/at dusk
(half mark)

WIDER PRACTICE

1   If tourism is a big issue in the area in which you are teaching, you could ask local tourist officials to talk to students about employment prospects, ways of managing tourism which respect the environment and heritage, and future tourism projects.

2   If you know of someone who has an unusual or exciting hobby activity, he/she could either come into the class to describe it and answer questions, or you could tape him or her talking about it and replay the talk for discussion. Sometimes a parent or relative of a student is delighted to be invited to share their experiences with the class.

3   If you have access to TV or radio in English, you may be able to record interesting programmes which reflect the unit's themes. Consumer holiday programmes are popular on British TV, and there is a growing emphasis on activity/adventure/special interest holidays. There could be many interesting spin offs: listening for factual detail, comparing places to stay, as well as adding to students' knowledge and understanding of all that the leisure industry involves.

4   Students might like to do a cross-curricular project in which they investigate a topic which draws on geography, history, literature or technology, etc and present it to the class. The following topics might give you some ideas:

•   An investigation into popular pastimes – their origins, how they are played, and reasons for their popularity

•   Any topic around the seven natural wonders of the world

•   An investigation into the history, design and decoration of any important buildings the students are curious about

•   Students could write to the embassy or tourist office of a country they are interested in, asking for information. Many organisations are very generous and will send all kinds of information about their country free of charge. Students could use this for writing a profile on the country.

•   They could investigate an ancient civilisation and trace its impact.

•   They could find out more about the history of their own language and make comparisons with English.

5   The travel theme lends itself well to the study of maps. Map reading is a very useful life skill, and the understanding of simple maps/location diagrams/ map symbols may be tested in the exam, so it is worth practising. (Students will not, however, be expected to interpret complex maps.)

Student Life

OVERVIEW

The main aim of this unit is to develop the skills students need for writing a letter of advice. Giving advice is a function that, particularly in written English, usually presents difficulties even for native speakers. This seems to be partly because the tone and the register are tricky to get right – subtle variations of tone can have a powerful impact on the effect of what is said, and there are important cultural differences between languages in terms of what is socially acceptable.

There is also a unit focus on the techniques which helps sustain an idea and develop it into a complete paragraph. This is one of the key areas where students need support if their hard work is going to translate into good exam grades.

The unit includes an analysis of tone and register in spoken English as part of a broader analysis of interactive techniques in conversation. This will help students become more familiar with the discourse strategies used in the Oral assessment. It will also, hopefully, improve classroom talk in general. In addition, there are opportunities for students to learn more about listening (there is an interview with a college counsellor) and understanding what they read (a magazine article on exam tension). Both these exercises, like the letters of advice, mirror the IGCSE exam format.

THEME

The unit is thematically linked through a number of topics of particular interest to young students. These include:

- leaving home to study – independence versus security
- coping with exam tensions and developing study skills
- making friends in a new environment
- responses to bullying.

The language study and themes have been selected to combine popular IGCSE topics with skills that are frequently tested.

There are many exercises in the unit. Why not use your insight into your particular class to really home in on those areas where development is needed, even if it means cutting other exercises short?

LANGUAGE WORK

The language work includes detailed work on useful phrases for asking for and giving advice, modals, and idiomatic expressions. Idioms are natural in informal contexts, students enjoy learning them, and they can greatly enhance the effectiveness of tone and register. Spelling and pronunciation focus on silent letters. Vocabulary is developed with more work on word building, and punctuation is revised.

Challenges of student life

1 Completing a checklist

The topic opens with a discussion about looking after yourself at university. If you feel this is culturally or socially very much outside students' likely experience, you may prefer to start off by getting them to think about transitional times in their life. Many students these days, even the youngest, have some experience of starting a new school, moving house for their parents' work, or settling in new neighbourhoods; some may have experience of boarding school. You may like to ask them to think about what has been good or difficult about that situation, and what they feel they have learned from it. With luck, you will be

able to elicit concepts relating to self-sufficiency, developing a larger range of social and practical skills, making new friends, relating to different kinds of people, understanding new rules, finding one's way around a strange area, etc.

Once understanding has been established, it will be helpful to use the pictures to set the scene about what is expected of a young person coping at university. If you have students who have already experienced being away from home to study or work, then it would be ideal to capitalise on their experience and let their views be your starting point.

After discussing the pictures, let students complete the checklist by themselves so as not to pre-empt the exercise on interactive techniques.

2 Before you listen: Interactive skills – 7 Comparing languages

The aim of this sequence of exercises is to increase students' understanding of the nuts and bolts of a lively conversation. The dialogue is a bit contrived, of course, but it will help them cope better with the Oral assessment and improve their classroom talk. Peter and Alison take an equal part in the conversation, whereas the teacher/interlocutor's role in the Oral is to manipulate the discourse so that students have the best possible opportunity to demonstrate their oral skills. Thus, ideally, the interlocutor says a lot less than the candidate. In oral pairwork in class, students sometimes tend to take turns saying their 'piece', listening to each other but not really interacting. The work on interactive skills will help them move on from this to greater fluency.

TAPESCRIPT

As in the Student's Book.

After they have read and listened to the dialogue, check that students really do understand the reasons why a warm tone is important. You might say something like *'Alison's an impulsive spender. She's afraid she might run out of money. Imagine how that feels.'* Whenever you see an opportunity, try to emphasise the importance of students putting themselves into the shoes of another person before giving advice. If they can do this (and it certainly comes easier to some students than to others, depending on their language resources and temperament) they will be halfway there in attaining a natural 'feel' for an appropriate tone and register.

If you share a common language with your students, it's a good idea to compare and contrast ways of offering advice in the two languages. Advice-giving in English is often understated and oblique. It may well be worth comparing the similarities and differences of tone and register between the two languages.

GIVING ADVICE ORALLY AND IN WRITING

Before moving on to the next sequence of exercises, which are based on giving advice in writing, it's useful to focus on the differences between giving advice orally and in writing. You may like to ask students how they perceive the differences. To make this clearer, you may find offering a dramatic example helps, e.g. *'A member of your family has been badly hurt on holiday. Would you prefer to hear the news in person or read about it in a letter? Why?'* Try to elicit from students the fact that bad news, as well as exceptionally good news such as winning the lottery, tends to be broken in person because the listener's reaction is unpredictable, and so the speaker needs more leeway. Elicit from students the unique elements of face-to-face contact: body language, the opportunity to smile/to look sorry/to tailor what we say to the person's reactions, the scope for the listener to ask questions. All these allow a flexibility which can never be attained in writing.

You can set up the following mini role plays as **extension activities** if you think it's appropriate:

- Your friend is keen to leave school and take a job but you feel he'd be wiser to stay on and get some qualifications. What do you say?

- A young man hoping to be promoted at his firm is rejected after an interview. He asks his manager for advice about how to do better next time. You are the manager. What do you say?

- Your sister wants to marry her boyfriend. You feel she is too young and the boy is unsuitable for her. What do you say?

8 Reading and discussing a problem letter

Before they begin reading, ask students to find out if the writer of the letter has difficulties at university that they anticipated for themselves. This will help them focus on the letter and provides continuity with the earlier work in the unit. The pairwork, after the letter, provides more opportunities to exploit and reinforce advice language.

9 Reading a model letter of reply

The model letter of reply demonstrates how a friendly but non-patronising tone can be achieved in a letter of advice. It is intended to serve as a reference point when students get deeper into the unit. Remind them that they can look back at this as an example of how an advice letter could be written.

It's important after the pairwork to get cross-class discussion and feedback on the model letter to make sure that there have been no misunderstandings.

ANSWERS

Students should underline these phrases:

A little tip I'd like to pass on is to …

Try to …

all you really have to do is …

why not …?

don't forget to …

It's not a good idea to …

You won't forget to …, will you?

10 Analysing the model letter

As this is a key exercise, you may prefer to monitor the discussion through a whole-class approach. Use this opportunity to ask students why the tone of the letter of reply is particularly tactful. Encourage them to think about how the writer, who has to express advice on paper, uses extra-tactful phrases to compensate for the fact that she is not able to give this advice face-to-face.

IGCSE candidates are not expected to take the role of anyone but themselves, or to write letters of advice that would be outside their range of experience. Emphasis in the exam is on an exchange of views between peers, and a relaxed and chatty tone and register will be rewarded.

11 Advice phrases

Many IGCSE candidates can make basic use of modals such as *should* and *must*. The exam, however, is looking for a more sophisticated handling of advice language. Candidates need to show a grasp of the nuances of meaning in the advice language they use. This exercise provides further practice in discriminating between registers and shades of tone and meaning. Eventually, with perseverance, your students will build up a repertoire of language for a variety of occasions where advice of some sort or other is needed.

Elicit from students the fact that intensifiers such as *absolutely* in '*You absolutely must*' make the advice much stronger. You could ask them to suggest alternatives to *absolutely*, such as *certainly, definitely, really*.

12 Expressing problems

The way we express our problems is linked to who we are and the culture we come from. It would be fascinating to hear students' views on the language they use to express problems in particular situations in their cultures.

You may like to highlight the indirectness of the informal statement *I'm not sure what to do*. This invites the listener to advise/suggest without asking directly for help. Advice/suggestions would then be offered in a seemingly casual and understated fashion, e.g. *I suppose you could always …*

If students are having difficulty thinking of problems, possible prompts are:

*   A mother is waiting for her young child to return from school. He/she is three hours late.

*   An expensive pair of shoes you bought ten days ago have completely fallen to pieces. On the receipt it says that faulty goods have to be returned within seven days.

*   You're talking to your friend about re-decorating your bedroom. You're undecided between re-doing the room in white or another colour.

*   You're on holiday in a foreign country. You know no-one and do not speak the language. You find that your bag with your passport and money have been stolen. What do you say when you telephone home?

13 Tone and register in students' letters

In this exercise, students study extracts from letters of advice. The extracts reveal typical weaknesses at IGCSE level: candidates struggle to convey ideas and attitudes with limited language resources. Their attempts to strike an intimate, informal note (praiseworthy though they are in their own way) have some hilarious effects.

The exercise is ideal for mixed ability work in small groups. More able students, who have a quicker 'feel' for tone and register, may enjoy helping weaker students, who tend to be more caught up with the basic meaning of the language and less sensitive to the nuances. Why not let the more able students lead the groups and take a back seat yourself?

Extract 5 is the most suitably written paragraph.

14 Rewriting a paragraph

Encourage students to rewrite one of the paragraphs they didn't like, with help if necessary.

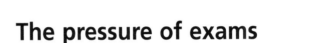

The pressure of exams

15 Pre-reading task

Before students do the activity, it would be useful to focus the whole class on the pressures exams cause by asking them how they feel about preparing for and taking exams. You could elicit their comments and jot them on the board. It will be interesting to see how your students' views compare with the opinions given in the Student's Book.

You could end this activity on a positive note by asking students whether it is possible to learn to enjoy taking exams. Some people say they enjoy exams because it gives them a chance to show what they can do and they are stimulated by the challenge.

16 Reading for gist

The magazine article comprises some interesting interviews with three students who are taking GCSE exams. By presenting not only the students' viewpoints, but also the mothers' and an expert's, it allow us to consider a variety of facets of the pressure exams place, not just on the student, but on the whole family. The article is sure to provoke some lively discussion.

The role of the 'expert' can be introduced here. The concept is developed further in the later listening exercise on the college counsellor (pages 128/9). You could ask '*What kind of background/ experience do you think the expert has?*'

17 Comprehension check

ANSWERS

1   The statements which are true for Sam are: b and c.
2   The statements which are true for Khalid are: b, c and d.

3 The statements which are true for Matthew are: a, c and d.

18 Post-reading discussion

It will be most intriguing to hear students' thoughts on Sam, Matthew and Khalid. The discussion is a valuable opportunity to draw out some cultural comparisons about styles of exams, approaches to study and family attitudes.

Particular issues to explore could be:

- Exams undoubtedly are stressful, but does stress have any positive effects? (You could elicit: it can spur you on to work harder/some students thrive in a competitive atmosphere/you appreciate and savour more fully times which are relaxing.)

- Is coursework (which is common in the UK, but may not be so elsewhere) a good idea, or can you end up overloaded?

- How can you build confidence for exams?

- How can the family help the student who is in the middle of exams?

19 Vocabulary: Colloquial words and phrases

Making suitable use of colloquialisms helps students achieve a good, informal tone. This exercise recycles words and phrases they met in the text.

ANSWERS

A 1 moan, put your foot down about it
2 exam nerves
3 stick to
4 working out
5 loads

B Other meanings:
moan: sound one makes when in pain
loads: large amounts of something carried/ transported etc
working out: calculating, being successful
stick to: adhere to (i.e. something sticky)

20 Word building

Students could use dictionaries for this word-building exercise. Encourage them to create sentences to show meanings, as this will test their understanding of how to use the words in context.

BUILDING NOUNS FROM VERBS: ANSWERS

appointment
astonishment
arrangement
entertainment
advertisement
improvement
management
disagreement

Other examples to elicit: *disappointment, postponement, enlargement, enjoyment, enhancement, encouragement.*

BUILDING ADJECTIVES FROM NOUNS: ANSWERS

magical
musical
classical
personal
cultural
functional
mathematical
natural

Other examples to elicit: *national, political, logical, emotional, recreational.*

You could extend this exercise by considering the suffix *-ful*. The examples *stressful* and *helpful* are found in the text. Other examples to elicit are: *colourful, useful, harmful, thoughtful, beautiful.* You could also ask students which of these words have an opposite with the suffix *-less* (all the above except *stressful* and *beautiful*).

21 Language study: Giving advice

Students have come across the sort of language the expert uses earlier in the unit. The aim of this exercise is to help them use their existing knowledge to further explore contrasts and similarities between advice expressions. It also encourages them to look for meaningful patterns in the grammar and helps them work out guidelines for using modals correctly.

The questions draw attention to the special features of modal auxiliaries. The main ideas to elicit are as follows.

ANSWERS

1 *Need(s) to* and *should* sound more indirect than *must*. Students might add that the expert uses a passive construction in **a** and **c**, which sounds less prescriptive than an active one. This would be a good comment.

2 *Need* is followed by the infinitive with *to. Must* and *should* are never followed by *to*

3 *Should* Khalid be encouraged …?

Does Khalid's mother *need to* …?

Do his parents *need to* …?

4 Khalid's mother *doesn't need to* …

Matthew's parents offer … *doesn't need to* be linked/*needn't* be linked …

His parents *don't need to/needn't* sit down …

5 *Ought to* can replace *should* and *need(s) to. Has to* can replace *must.*

22 *Should/shouldn't have*

Should/shouldn't have + past participle express blame and criticism of your own or another's actions. They are very direct, so students need to be careful of the way they use the structures when addressing people.

PRACTICE: ANSWERS

1   Joseph shouldn't have taken a part-time job when he had exams coming up.
2   Trudi shouldn't have gone to the concert when she had an exam the next day.
3   He should have checked his bank balance before he spent a lot of money.
4   I shouldn't have shouted at my brother when he was trying to be helpful.
5   I shouldn't have borrowed my sister's jacket without asking her first.
6   You should have bought some extra bread when you knew we needed to make sandwiches.

23 Using a more informal tone

ANSWERS

1   I don't need to cook as Damian is taking us out for a meal.
    (Student Book should read: It *isn't* necessary for me to cook …)
2   You should/ought to/need to do your homework at a regular time each evening.
3   You shouldn't/oughtn't to have made a promise you can't keep.
4   I shouldn't/oughtn't to have left all my revision to the last minute.
5   Abdul must/had better get some rest or he will fail his exams.
6   I should/ought to have listened to her advice.
7   He shouldn't/oughtn't to have played computer games instead of revising for the exam.

You could round off this exercise on register by asking students to consider the underlying strength of emotion in this kind of statement:

I'm a bit annoyed, I must say.

This is a typical English understatement and native speakers hearing it would guess that the speaker was angry about something. This is shown particularly by the phrase *I must say*. Contexts in which you might make this comment could be:

Your friend returns a book he/she borrowed from you and you find that several pages are torn.

You pay quite a lot of money for a second-hand bicycle which the previous owner assures you is in very good condition. After a few days you detect a lot of faults.

24 Spelling and pronunciation: Silent letters

Silent letters are often the cause of spelling errors – students can't hear them so they don't include them in words they write.

Before beginning the exercise, you could write a word, e.g. *castle*, on the board and ask if all the letters in it are pronounced. When you have established that *t* is silent, you could ask for other examples. These could be categorised according to particular letters.

Some possibilities are:

silent l   –   *chalk, palm, would*
silent c   –   *muscles, scene*
silent p   –   *pneumonia, psychology*
silent w –   *sword, wreath, who*
silent k   –   *knot, kneel, knight*
silent g   –   *design, reign, gnat*
silent gh –   *straight, bought, caught*
silent t   –   *thistle, fasten, soften*
silent h   –   *exhaustion, vehicle, heir*

Monitor students' pronunciation as they practise saying the words aloud.

25 Crossing out silent letters

ANSWERS

1g **2**w **3**h **4**w **5**gh **6**c **7**l **8**l **9**u **10**g **11**gh **12**h

Elicit other examples of words with these silent letters.

26 Adding silent letters

ANSWERS

1   drought
2   talk
3   Would, biscuit
4   Whereabouts
5   half, whole
6   write, answers
7   lights
8   wrist, knee
9   white
10 Honesty
11 scent
12 whistle, wrong
13 wrote, pseudonym
14 reigned
15 psychic

27 Detecting patterns

The aim of this exercise is to help students use what they already know about silent letters to come to conclusions about meaningful regularities. This will help them with pronunciation when they come across unfamiliar words, and with spelling.

They might need some help to detect patterns, so you could start with an example. You could write *psychic* on the board and ask them to think of other words which start with *ps* (e.g. *psychiatrist, psychology, psalm*). Make sure students are clear that when the letters *ps* come at the beginning of a word, the *p* is silent.

Other patterns students might notice and which help towards rule formation are:

pn at the beginning of words has a silent *p*: *pneumonia*, *pneumatic*.

gn usually has a silent *g*: *design*, *assign*, *gnat*.

wr has a silent *r*: *write*, *wrap*, *wrong*.

wh has an almost completely silent *h* in question words (except *who*): *what*, *which*, *why*, *when*, *where* and in the numerous other words beginning with *wh*: *white*, *wheel*, *whisper* etc.

st usually has a silent *t* when followed by *l* or *e*: *whistle*, *fasten*.

As always, it is illuminating for students to compare and contrast patterns in their own language(s) with English patterns. You could encourage them to reflect on any illogicalities they have noticed and to share these with others.

28 Idiomatic expressions

The words containing silent letters are: *hustle*, *bustle*, *light*, *limb*,

29 Look, say, cover, write, check

Using a visual strategy will help students recall the actual 'look' of words which use silent letters.

Studying effectively

30 Punctuation reminders

These punctuation reminders will help weaker students and provide revision for more proficient ones.

The topic is homework which ties in with the study skills theme in general. Homework is not universal, so it's a good idea to make sure students understand what it actually is, if necessary. Elicit their approach to tackling homework – you could make a list of tips on the board. Questions to raise can include:

- Should the TV or radio be on during homework time?

- How long should you spend on homework?

- What should you do if you can't understand your homework?

- Should you work at a desk/table?

- What time should you start your homework?

- Is it right to get help from parents or friends to complete homework?

ANSWER

I need a few quiet moments to myself when I get in from school. I have a drink and relax for a while. Then I get out my homework. I work at a desk in the corner of the living room. It is peaceful but not silent. I like French and maths homework the best.

I've got a few reference books which I keep on a shelf above my desk. I borrow my brother's paints for artwork and I use my mum's computer for GCSE coursework. I've used my dad's tools for some technology projects too. They don't mind me borrowing their things as long as I take care of them.

Our school, Cardiff High, has a homework hotline. This means that you can telephone the school to check the homework you've been set. It also stops teachers setting too many subjects for homework at once. About two years ago, I had English, history, German, physics, biology, maths and technology homework on the same night. It was a nightmare. The homework hotline prevents these problems. However, it also means teaches refuse to accept silly excuses for not handing in homework.

31 Rewriting a letter

In this exercise, as well as deciding on paragraphing, students are asked to analyse the tone and register. First they need to disentangle the actual sense of the letter. Then they should work out the writer's intention (to console and advise), and discuss why he does not succeed in achieving a suitable tone.

To help focus on improving the tone, ask students to picture the situation and to imagine how Harry, who has failed an exam most of his friends have passed, is feeling. Ask them questions along the lines of: '*Will he want to be preached at? To be reproached? To be made to feel small? Have you ever been in a similar position? Can you remember what it felt like?*' Aim to elicit the need for a sympathetic but controlled response which focuses on what Harry can do, rather than his failings. This involves leaving out anything that could be interpreted as a reproach or a slur on his intelligence.

The letter will, hopefully, get a few smiles, which is a good response. Encourage students to decide what's worth saving and what they should discard, and let them discuss suitable alternative phrases, e.g. *I'm keeping my fingers crossed for you.*

MODEL ANSWER

This model is just one possible answer, which students may like to compare with their own.

Dear Harry,

I was really sorry to hear that you're unable to join us on the trip because you have to resit your exam. You must be feeling really fed up and I do sympathise with you.

It might be a good idea to contact Toby, as I know he is resitting too. How about revising together? I'm sure he'd be glad of your support and companionship.

An approach I found helpful which you may like to try is to get hold of the syllabus and underline the relevant sections. I know you've probably done this (if so ignore me), but I found checking past papers to identify typical questions helped a lot. There's a lot of time pressure in the exam, so it's definitely worth practising the answers in the specified time.

Let me know as soon as you get your results. I'll be keeping my fingers crossed for you. We'll miss you a lot on holiday and it won't be the same without you.

Lots of love,

Oscar

32 Reading aloud

Students can try out the effect of the tone and register they have achieved on a small audience.

33 More idiomatic expressions

Before students start the exercise it's worth making sure they understand the literal meaning of the component words of the idioms.

It's interesting to encourage students to relate the idioms to similar ones in their own language. If the class is monolingual and you share the students' language, you are well placed to encourage some very heated debate!

ANSWERS

1a 2b 3c 4d 5b 6b 7a

34 Increasing your stock of idioms

Using idioms effectively is obviously more difficult than just understanding them. You'll need to emphasise that idioms have a precise meaning and are only applicable in specific situations. Misapplied idioms can have some hilarious results! You might like to ask students to keep records of those idioms they like and to use them as much as possible until they are really sure they know the appropriate contexts for them.

35 Sentence correction

These sentences, which are taken from students' actual writing, are quite challenging to rewrite. Students may like to treat them as problem-solving exercises, working on them together to identify the intended meaning and then rephrasing them.

POSSIBLE ANSWERS

1 You would be wise to / If I were you I'd follow your teacher's advice.
2 Try to develop a positive attitude to / frame of mind for your work.
3 Remember that a good friend can be a tremendous help.
4 Whatever you do, you should never take drugs / you should avoid drugs – they bring a lot more pain than pleasure.
5 Many people would agree with the points in your letter.

INTERNATIONAL OVERVIEW

As always, it is worth checking basic understanding of what has been read in the extract, just to make sure that your class has assimilated the facts. For example, you could ask students what percentage of nine-year-olds in Singapore and England did homework once a week at the age of nine.

Styles of teaching and learning vary a lot across the world. Find out how students like to learn things. Ask if they prefer to study in classes where there is a lot of freedom and emphasis on group work and problem-solving, or in more structured classes where everyone is taught in the same way at the same pace.

A range of advice

36 Pre-listening tasks

Going to a counsellor is becoming more popular in the West. Before you start the exercises, you might like to stimulate an open discussion by writing on the board:

'Counselling – the biggest growth industry of the nineties!'

Clarify the concept of 'counsellor' so everyone has a general understanding, and then ask students to comment on why counselling is booming in certain countries. You may be able to elicit ideas such as: greater family mobility means separation from older relatives who people used to turn to with problems; competitive, go-getting societies put more strain on individuals making them feel stressed and in need of support; there is a high rate of family breakdown in some countries.

Students can then do A and B in groups or pairs, and give feedback to the whole class. Possible disadvantages of counsellors include the difficulty of checking their credentials, the difficulty of knowing whether any advice is indeed sound, the risk of becoming dependent on counselling, the expense if you have to pay.

37 Listening for gist: A college counsellor

After you have played the tape once for gist listening, ask students if the questions they wrote have been answered.

TAPESCRIPT

Listen to the interview. Which of the questions that you wrote are answered?

INTERVIEWER: What are some typical problems students bring to you?
COUNSELLOR: A very common one is, um, not having enough finance to get through college, um, getting into debt. And they come needing advice.
I: How can you help?

C: We break down their spending and see if there are any economies – moving to a cheaper flat near the college saves rent, and travel costs, um, for instance. We also talk about funds they can tap into like, for instance, outside agencies that can give small grants ... and I help them write letters. The college itself has a hardship fund they can apply to.

I: Is that reasonably successful?

C: Yes, it helps, but as a counsellor I'm also concerned that financial problems bring about other problems. So I look at whether needing financial assistance is putting an extra strain on their personal relationships.

I: Are there other times when problems seem to peak?

C: Before exams. Er, maybe they're finding exams stressful, they're worried they can't retain information ... it ... it just goes, and they get mental blocks leading to being stressed in the exam period.

I: What do you offer?

C: I do things like study techniques, summarising their notes very briefly into key words. I emphasise that, you know, quality is better than quantity: do a bit at a time, but really try to take it in. Relaxation and exercise are important, too, in helping them to cope. I try and see if there are underlying problems. I mean, why should exams be a problem now if they've done all right before? Is something in their personal lives worrying them and, you know, we get them to talk about those things as well.

I: I see you normally are prepared to go quite deeply into things?

C: It depends. For example, if young people are still living with their parents and, um, they don't feel they're listened to, that their needs are not catered for, then we need to tackle that. I get the ... the rest of the family to come and see me, too. And I help students to say how they feel to their parents. One problem, for instance, might be overcrowding, having to share a bedroom, that sort of thing, and I suggest ways that a student can get more space and privacy at home.

I: So you look at each case in an individual light?

C: As a counsellor I think it's very important to make them feel comfortable, not be judgmental. Everything is confidential – I don't discuss a student's problems with anyone else without their permission. Unless ... well, there is one main exception ... something illegal is involved. Good quality counselling can't happen without trust.

I: So you would never openly criticise what a student is doing?

C: I try to get away from being critical. Often students have suffered too much from that. The most straightforward cases are where people want clear advice, for example, on choosing the best course for them, but counselling is not quite like that. In my view, it's primarily about supporting people who are confused or unhappy to explore their own issues. What they're going through now may be linked back to bad childhood experiences, for instance. It's ... it's no good me just telling them what to do – it's essential they see things for themselves.

I: In general, how do you cope with what must be a fairly draining kind of job?

C: We see so many people! We always have appointments unless it's an emergency. This allocates a set amount of time to each student. And, um, it helps if you remember you're not responsible for their problems. Only they can, ultimately, make changes in their lives. I couldn't afford to be any other way. I'd be swamped!

38 Detailed listening

 Let students listen again to answer the comprehension questions. Check the answers by pausing the tape in the right places.

In the exam, the occasional spelling or grammar mistake in a candidate's answers will not matter as long as the answers are unambiguous and communicated clearly.

ANSWERS

1 Any two of the following are acceptable:
Reduce their living costs.
Move to a cheaper flat to save money on rent and travelling.
Apply to outside agencies for financial help.
Apply to the college hardship fund.

2 She wants to find out if they have other personal problems or worries which are actually the cause of the exam stress.

3 She might ask the family to take part in a discussion with the student present, and help the student say how she feels.

4 If something illegal was happening.

5 Because counselling is concerned with getting people to explore/think about their own problems in their own way.

6 She doesn't think of herself as being responsible for other people's problems.

Note that the above answers are given very fully for clarity. In the exam, listening answers can be extremely brief. The important thing for students to convey is accuracy of understanding, so even a brief note can be enough to attract the mark if it covers the key information.

39 Rewriting a letter of advice

Before students dive into rewriting the letter with a more tactful tone and register, encourage them to consider the problem and what could be done about it.

MODEL ANSWER

This is a possible version of the letter, for students to compare with their own attempts.

Dear Roberto

I was sorry to hear that you are having a tough time getting on with your little brother. I know small children can be very annoying and it's not an easy problem to resolve.

My younger brother, Tom, used to drive me up the wall. Like your brother, he was always interfering with my things and even damaging them. I used to get bad-tempered and impatient with him, and we often had a strained atmosphere at home. Eventually, I decided to discuss the problem with my parents and, to my surprise, they saw my point of view. Thomas now agrees not to touch my things, and anything really precious I put somewhere he cannot reach it.

Nowadays we get on quite well. I play football with him and give him a hand with his homework. He has become more of a friend than an enemy. Do you think this approach could work for you? You could always give it a try.

Looking forward to hearing from you.

All the best,

Crispin

40 Building a letter from a list of points

The main challenge in this exercise is for students to select some relevant points from the list given. They need to work on expanding a few points with more detail so that they achieve interesting, well-developed paragraphs. Writing out a bald list of points won't show the maturity of expression the exam is looking for.

After they have brainstormed some ideas of their own about how to resolve the problem, you could take one point from the list and show how it could be expanded with interesting details or examples.

For example:

It's a good idea not to leave it too late in the evening to start your homework. For example, I usually prefer to have a short rest and a snack when I get in from school, and then get down to it. I concentrate better earlier on, and I have the rest of the evening free to relax or see friends. If you start your homework late, you may find you have to stay up late to finish it, which makes you feel tired the next day.

41 Pre-writing discussion

Bullying is introduced as a fresh topic for discussion. You could ask students whether bullying is a problem only for younger children, or whether it can happen in other contexts, e.g. between workmates, among teenagers, and what causes it.

It will be interesting to hear students' ideas on what could be done to resolve the problem. There are no simple formulas to prevent or cure bullying. Some ideas to elicit, which could be adapted for the letter of advice in the next exercise, are:

- Bullying is wrong and must be stopped.
- The victim must report the bullying to someone in authority.
- The victim is not to blame and shouldn't feel guilty.
- Adults must take responsibility to resolve the problem.
- They should make sure the bully understands that his/her behaviour is at fault and must be changed.
- Bullies are often inadequate people and bully others to cover up their sense of inferiority.

- A meeting between bully and victim, when each listens to the other's point of view, can be productive.
- Some schools set bully and victim to work on a joint project so they can get to know each other as individuals – this has been shown to have positive results.

42 Letter completion

This exercise offers more much-needed practice in sustaining ideas and developing them into interesting paragraphs. You may wish to suggest students turn back to the model letter in exercise 9 for guidance.

Exam-format questions

Writing

In the writing section of the exam, different kinds of prompts are given to guide students along the right lines. It is important that they read the rubrics carefully. In Part 3, exercise 1, students are intended to use each prompt. This is indicated by an instruction like: *'Write a letter in which you should …'*, with a list of points to be covered in the answer. (See page 115 of the Student's Book for an example.)

However, in Part 3, exercise 3 (and sometimes in exercise 2) only *some* of the rubric prompts should be used. This is shown by phrases such as *'You may use the ideas below but you are free to add your own ideas'*, or *'The following may give you some ideas but you are free to add ideas of your own'*. In this case, candidates should be selective about their choice of prompts, and the best candidates choose two or more of the prompts and develop them into well rounded paragraphs. If all the prompts are used slavishly in this situation, the result is a 'list' with very superficial treatment of each idea, attracting a lower mark.

The exam-format questions on page 131 of the Student's Book are intended to encourage selectivity. The prompts which the students select should be expanded upon in the way they have practised earlier in the unit.

WIDER PRACTICE

1   If students are interested enough in the theme, you may like to invite an ex-pupil who speaks English well, and now attends a university, to visit the class and give them his/her opinions of university life.

Similarly, university officials (students' union officers, careers advisers, lecturers, welfare officers) could be invited to answer students' queries.

2   Developing insight into the subtleties of tone and register needs to be ongoing. It's nice to bring humour where you can into the examples you use. English newspapers, if available, can provide good examples of tone and register. Media treatment of the royal family is a good topic to choose. It's a perennial favourite in the British press, which is ever-ready with advice about how the royals should conduct themselves. Some years ago, for example, Princess Margaret was admitted to hospital with a smoking-related complaint. The chummy tabloid headline '*Give 'em up, Mag!*' could be contrasted with the broadsheet comment '*Princess Margaret advised to restrict cigarette consumption*'.

3   You may like to collect further examples of letters which contrast tone and register. A formal register, using longer words of Latin origin, passive forms and no contractions, could be contrasted with the short, sharp, active style of informal registers.

You could present students with a situation, perhaps a dispute between neighbours about noise levels. Ask one group to imagine that they have no wish to fall out with their neighbours. They should write a note to the neighbours explaining the problem and asking politely for more peace and quiet. The other group should read the letter and take offence. They seek legal advice and send a reply, particularly frozen in its tone and register, to their neighbours.

4   You could set up role plays and ask students to imagine they are addressing very different groups of people (e.g. small children, adults) on the same topic. Encourage them to adjust their tone and register to their audience.

Topics could include:

- keeping our neighbourhood clean (picking up litter, etc)
- road safety
- the importance of a healthy diet.

BACKGROUND INFORMATION
State education in the UK

- Children go to primary school between $4\frac{1}{2}$ and 11 years, and to secondary or comprehensive school from 11 years to 16 or 18. The minimum school-leaving age is 16.

- Many young people continue their education between 16 and 18 at school or sixth-form college. (Sixth-form college is only for those aged 16 to 18.)

- In some areas, children go to primary school until age 9, middle school from 9 to 13, and upper school from 13 onwards.

- Further education colleges offer a wide range of courses, both vocational and academic, from the age of 16 onwards.

- Young people can go to university from the age of 18. They need to achieve a good standard of secondary education to be allowed entry.

- The principal exams taken are normally GCSEs at age 16, and GCSE A-levels (Advanced levels) at age 18. Most pupils take A-levels in only three subjects.

(*Note: Scotland has a different education system from the rest of the United Kingdom.*)

EXAMPLE OF LIKELY EXAM GRADING
Letter of advice

Dear David

Hello! I heard you are on holidays for three weeks! Lucky you! In your letter you seemed rather unhappy in your new school. Well I'll tell you one thing if any of us back here would be better off than here in this old school, we're all sick of it, at least you have a chance of meeting new people and have a new school. I think all you need is a bit more time to settle down and decide who you want to be with. You told me that you are bored during the wekends, so you should join a club or something you are good in volley ball and swimming, I think you should also start looking in a part-time job so we can go abroad together during the summertime. Well, I have got to start with my homework soon, please take time and think about my suggestions, hope to hear from you soon.

Lots of love,

Yours sincerely

This sort of answer would receive about 8 out of 12 marks, putting it in the C category.

Happy Endings

This unit focuses on narrative technique. Writing a story features regularly in the essay-writing questions in the exam. Students are expected to use their imagination to build a story around something that could conceivably happen in their real lives. They can expect a wide variety of stimuli in the exam, e.g. recounting an incident on a journey, losing something, a burglary, a storm, an accident, a fire. They are usually given a 'scenario' to work from which gives them a brief outline of what happened.

THEME

A sea theme has been chosen for this unit because it can provide the key ingredients for a good story: heroism, adventure, rescue missions, drama etc. It's a popular IGCSE topic, and comprehension of sea-related issues has often been tested.

Areas for discussion, which are relevant to other aspects of the exam including Oral Assessment, are:

- Why are people so fascinated by the sea?
- What do we mean when we talk about 'heroism?'
- How can negative experiences, which cause hardship and struggle, be turned into something positive so that we ultimately come to benefit from them?
- Is the desire for adventure also a wish for greater self-knowledge and personal development?
- What lessons can be learned from dangerous or frightening events?

LANGUAGE WORK

Structuring a narrative means ordering the events coherently and making the links between events clear. Whilst most IGCSE students will have met the narrative tenses they need to use before, 'putting them all together' still presents a challenge. The unit deals with this through exercises analysing how and why narratives work, and through follow-up activities.

Students who show they have a wide vocabulary and can manipulate structures to dramatic effect will be rewarded. The unit helps students build up these skills by vocabulary expansion exercises, using emotional and dramatic language, and writing more complex sentences. Reported speech, which students will probably already have met, is revised.

The call of the sea

1 Visualisation

Let students have as much time as they need for the visualisation so that they can freely associate with any aspect of the sea which comes into their mind. Writing down what they visualised might best be done in their own language.

2 Discussion

Students compare statements encompassing the romantic and adventurous aspects of the sea with their own views. Many of the ideas are followed up in greater detail later in the unit, so it's useful to hear students' views and encourage them to be as speculative as possible.

3 Sea vocabulary: Odd word out

The vocabulary work prepares for many of the lexical items later in the unit. It's a good idea to remind students to make a note in their vocabulary records of unfamiliar words.

ANSWERS

hive	tram
spanner	solicitor
squirrel	abseiling

4 Sea vocabulary: Onomatopoeic words

A You could demonstrate onomatopoeic sounds by taking some noisy things into the class, e.g. a bag of crisps, a bunch of keys, and eliciting onomatopoeic words, e.g. *rustle, crackle, jangle, rattle.*

ANSWERS

boats: hooting
waves: lapping, roaring, crashing, slapping, splashing
seagulls: screeching
wind: roaring, howling
mud: squelching

B Other words students might know are:
bang, crack, tick, pop, creak, jingle, hum, squeak, whistle, sizzle, whine, tap.

C It's very interesting for everyone if students give examples of onomatopoeic words in their own language(s).

5 Writing a descriptive paragraph / 6 Reading aloud

Students consolidate this stage of learning by writing a descriptive paragraph and reading it aloud to their groups for comments. As always, encourage positive feedback and constructive criticism.

7 Pre-reading discussion

The sea has always been important to Britain's identity. Its imperial power was built on its naval strength. The sea is a potent symbol of independence and plays a large part in British cultural traditions. It's interesting to learn from students what part the sea plays in the history of their own country.

Tell students a bit about *Robinson Crusoe*, written by Daniel Defoe, and published in 1719. Based on the true story of Alexander Selkirk, a Scottish sailor, it is a fully developed narrative and has been called the first proper English novel.

The idea of a castaway on a desert island fending completely for himself really seized the public imagination and the book was an immediate success. Many subsequent stories, films and radio programmes have hinged on this concept.

8 Reading and sequencing

Before they begin reading, you could ask students to predict the content. They could discuss what makes a good story, e.g. strong characterisation, powerful scenes, dramatic incidents, an intriguing or fast-moving plot. If appropriate, encourage them to use insights they are gaining in other parts of the curriculum, e.g. from the study of literature.

ANSWERS

The order of events in the story is:

1i 2c 3e 4a 5k 6h 7j 8b 9f 10g 11d

9 Comprehension check

ANSWERS

1   Crusoe's father wanted him to be a lawyer.
2   He survived storms, was taken as a slave, had a plantation in Brazil.
3   Crusoe's cry 'Am I all alone?' emphasises his sense of isolation.
4   To salvage everything of value
5   He lived in a civilised way, he grew crops, he looked after his animals.
6   A footprint
7   A ship arrived which had been taken over by mutineers. They landed on the island. Crusoe trapped them and freed the captain, who took him to England.

10 Language study: Narrative tenses

The idea of this exercise is to help students use the grammatical knowledge they already have and apply it to the study of tenses in the Robinson Crusoe text.

The difficulty for many students at this level is not in understanding the theory of tenses or the underlying rules (they're often very accurate when doing drills in grammar books), but in applying their knowledge in different situations. Seeing how tenses are used in authentic texts is a dependable way to reinforce and extend understanding, which they can then build on in their own writing.

You could pair a weaker with a more able student for the exercise if you think it would help.

After students have worked out their own ideas for formation and usage, you could open up the discussion to the whole class. Why not ask an able student to record notes on the board?

THE PAST SIMPLE
The past simple of regular verbs is formed by adding *-ed* or *-d*, e.g. *I joined a big trading ship.* Exceptions include: *was, knew, ran, found.*

The past simple is common in story telling as it shows one completed action or event following another and it moves the story forward. Paragraphs 6 and 7 of the story contain good examples.

THE PAST CONTINUOUS
The past continuous is formed with *was/were* and the *-ing* form of the verb, e.g. *I was breaking my father's heart.*

It is used for actions in progress in the past, often interrupted by another action, e.g. *He was escaping the anger of his countrymen and I gave him refuge.*

In story telling it is often used for background information and descriptions setting the scene. You could extend the discussion by eliciting a further example such as:

It seemed like any other ordinary day at the market. Stallholders were selling fruit and vegetables, shoppers were buying food for the weekend, dogs were barking and children were playing near the fountain. I was walking towards the café to meet a friend when I noticed a strange object lying on the ground....

THE PAST PERFECT
The past perfect is formed with *had* + the past participle, e.g. *I had always wanted to go to sea.*

It is used to show that something had already happened at the point in time we are talking about, before another action, e.g. *I sowed barley I had taken from the ship.*
The captain had been taken prisoner.

Once the earlier point in time is established, we don't need to keep using the past perfect simple – it's more natural to use the past simple.

THE 'FUTURE IN THE PAST'
This is formed with structures normally used to talk about the future but with the verb forms in the past. For example, *is going to* becomes *was going to, will come* becomes *would come.*

It is used when we are talking about the past, to refer to something that was still in the future at that time, e.g. *Friday was going to accompany me to England.*

Other examples which you could discuss are:

I went to the school reunion last week. I felt strange as I waited for everyone to turn up. I couldn't believe I was going to meet all my old school friends again.

I hoped I would have a chance to make a phone call during the meeting but we were too busy.

I visited the church where my brother was to be married.

11 Beginnings and endings

The beginning of the Robinson Crusoe text gives us a lot of information in two short paragraphs, which get us quickly into the action of the story. The last paragraph clearly brings his sojourn on the island to a definite end.

In the opening two paragraphs the tenses are present perfect, present simple, past simple passive, past perfect simple, past simple, past continuous and past simple. The verbs in the last paragraph are in the past simple.

12 Discussion: Heroism

A It will be interesting to hear what students think are the qualities of a hero or heroine. Possible answers in relation to Crusoe could be:

He makes the best of his situation – he has no self-pity or bitterness.
He lives with dignity, courage and self-reliance.
He treats Friday with respect and never tries to exploit him.
He's brave when he rescues the captain.

B For this part of the discussion you could ask: *'Is it only people faced with extraordinary problems who can be called heroic? Can ordinary people who show exceptional qualities be called heroic too, e.g. people with disabilities who manage to succeed against the odds, elderly people who lose a partner and face old age alone?'*

C Encourage students to give examples of their own heroes and heroines. Ask them to identify the qualities/attributes which make them heroic. You could say something like *'In what way would you like to be like your hero? How could you achieve that ideal?'*

D The discussion could then be extended along these lines: *'How can we benefit from 'ordinary' struggles in our everyday life? For example, you may have something in your life which seems negative, perhaps not getting on with a brother or sister, or finding a school subject, which is compulsory, very difficult. How can a negative experience be of value so that in the end it becomes positive?'*

It will be fascinating to hear students' responses. They may come up with ideas like:

We can learn more about ourselves and so understand other people better.
We can learn to empathise with people who have problems.
We can learn persistence – the importance of not giving up.

E Examples of things he might have learned from Friday are: a knowledge of herbs for treating illnesses etc, human values – no knowledge of money so no greed for material things.

13 Continuing a story creatively

Let students identify with Crusoe and think through the possibilities. After such a long time away, will anyone remember him? What is likely to have changed? How will Crusoe's experiences have changed him? Is he now better prepared for the real world, or has he been disadvantaged by his unique experience?

14 Writing from notes

ANSWER

We were standing on the deck of the ship when the captain said the English coast was in sight. I felt very strange. Was I really going to see England again? After so many years of solitude, the noise, bustle and crowds (or: the noise and bustle of the crowds) at/on the dock almost overwhelmed me. I was walking towards (the) town when I heard a voice call my name. I turned and saw my sister. She embraced me warmly. I knew from the tears in her eyes (that) she had forgiven me for hurting our parents. She told me she had been waiting for me since the day I left. She had almost given up hope when she got the message (that) I was alive.

15 Comparing cultures

You may prefer to ask students to research a favourite story, perhaps one from their childhood, for homework and then present it to the group.

16 Showing surprise: Stress and intonation

 In *wh-* questions the sentence normally has a falling intonation, with the main stress towards the end:

When did you arrive?

However, when we want to show surprise, the voice rises and the question word is stressed instead:

When did you arrive?

Let students listen carefully to the examples and have a chance to hear the contrasts. When the question is first asked, the stress and intonation are normal. When the question is repeated, the speaker shows surprise and wants clarification.

Pause the tape after each question and let students practise the intonation patterns. Finally, they can make up questions and answers of their own.

TAPESCRIPT

As in the Student's Book.

Adrift on the Pacific

17 Pre-listening tasks

Students are going to listen to an interview with a couple, Maurice and Vita, who attempted to sail in their own boat from England to New Zealand. Unfortunately, the boat was hit by a sperm whale and it sank. They were able to bale out and survived for several months on a life raft before they were rescued. The couple's courage and dignity come across on the tape, and it is a powerful tale of endurance.

VOCABULARY CHECK: ANSWERS

1 emigrate F
2 adrift B
3 counter-current E
4 improvise C
5 emaciated A
6 malnourished G
7 oblivious to D

NARRATIVE QUESTIONS

Remind students that a complete narrative should answer the questions *Who, What, Where, Why, How* and *When*.

To help them focus on the content of the story, students make up questions beginning with the above words before they listen, e.g.

What happened?
Why did you want to sail to New Zealand?
Where did the boat sink?
How did you survive?
Who rescued you?
When did you return to England?

Briefly revise the past tense question forms if you think it's necessary.

18 Detailed listening

 Let students listen to the tape once and find answers to their own questions.

TAPESCRIPT

Listen to the interview with the couple who survived. Try to note down answers to the questions you wrote.

INTERVIEWER: Why were you making the trip?
MAURICE: Well, Vita and I had decided to emigrate from England to New Zealand in our 32 foot boat, The Sandpiper.
I: When did disaster strike?

VITA: We left Southampton in June and we were near Panama in the Pacific Ocean when what we had often dreaded actually happened. Our boat was hit by a 40 foot sperm whale. A small hole appeared in the hull and she began to fill with water.
I: How long did the boat take to sink?
M: It took an hour to go down.
I: How did you react? I'm sure I'd have been petrified!
M: Well, er, actually there was no panic. We sort of went onto automatic and um, did all the right things. As experienced sailors, I suppose we were prepared for this sort of emergency. We had just enough time to get out onto a life raft and we found ourselves adrift in an ocean covering a third of the earth's surface.
I: What did you do first?
M: Oh, for the first three days we rowed towards the Galapagos Islands. With hindsight this was not such a great idea because it was exhausting work and we used up most of our energy and water supplies.
I: So what happened then?
V: We felt increasingly desperate. We headed for the equatorial counter-current that we hoped would take us to the Central American coast. We continued towards that coast for three weeks. Then, to our horror, a hostile current dragged us back out to the middle of the ocean.
I: How did you actually manage to cope with being stuck on a life raft?
M: The raft was 4 foot 6 inches – just small enough for us to sit on! We lived and slept where we sat. We were completely confined. It was like being in a tiny prison cell.
I: What did you eat?
M: We fished over the side, grabbing turtles, birds and sharks with our bare hands or improvising fishing lines. We became emaciated and malnourished. At times it seemed death was not far away.
V: There was absolute silence on the ocean – apart from the lap of the waves or the screeching of the gulls. It was eerie. Sometimes the sea was very rough. The waves crashed around us and the dinghy which we were towing kept flipping over.
I: Did you see any ships?
M: Only eight ships passed us all the time we were adrift. The first seven sailed by oblivious to us. We fired flares, waved and set fire to our clothes in turtle shells. Nothing attracted them.
I: So when did you actually see the boat that rescued you?
V: After 119 days adrift. We'd spent about 45 days without seeing a ship. Then I heard something. I told Maurice I thought I'd heard the engine of a boat and he thought I was going mad. But I shouted and the boat turned towards us.
M: The relief was overwhelming! We knew for the first time since the disaster the joy of being alive.
I: Who actually picked you up?
V: We were rescued by South Korean fishermen and returned to Britain a month later. We were so weak and ill it took five more months before we could walk properly.
M: And it took another nine months before we felt really well.
I: What actually kept you going when there was little hope of rescue?
M: We took it one day at a time. If we'd really thought about what might happen, we might have been overwhelmed. We just concentrated on staying alive. Hour by hour. Day by day.
I: Do you have any plans to get to New Zealand?
M: No. But we still love the sea so we've settled on the Isle of Wight.

19 Checking your answers

 Students can discuss the answers to their own questions.

20 Listening and note taking

Students should now listen again and complete the notes.

POSSIBLE ANSWERS

a They were emigrating to New Zealand.
b Near Panama in Pacific Ocean. Hit by sperm whale.
c Didn't panic. Got onto life raft.
d It was exhausting. Used up energy and water.
e Very small and cramped.
f Turtles, birds, sharks, fish.
g 119 days.
h Vita shouted.
i 5 months to walk properly, 9 more months to feel well.
j Took one day at a time.

21 Discussion: Motivation and adventure

A Each year many people take part in risky expeditions to climb mountains, cross seas, etc. It's fascinating to discuss with students all the issues raised and to hear their views. You could discuss the extreme mental resolution required, and hardships undertaken out of choice rather than necessity.

Possible questions could be:

Are they in search of a dream?

Do they want fame and success?

Are they egged on by group dynamics to do more and more risky things?

Are they afraid of failure and letting people down?

Are spiritual goals important – do they want to discover their own inner potential and limitations when put to extreme tests?

Are they bored and dissatisfied with ordinary life?

You could ask which of these ideas, if any, students would apply to Maurice and Vita.

B The discussion is now extended to consider the wider implications of adventurous projects.

You could round off the discussion by asking whether it's possible to develop as a person and build inner strength in ordinary circumstances, or whether it's necessary to go to extremes to do it.

22 Ordering events

It's a good idea to revise the use of time expressions by putting a few examples on the board and checking that students understand their function:

I'll ring you as soon as the letter arrives.
Is he going to ring a long time after, or just after the letter arrives?

He waited until the rain stopped before going out.
Did he go out when it was raining?

ANSWERS

The boxes should be numbered as follows:

2, 5, 6, 4, 7, 8, 10, 11, 9, 3, 1

The statements could be linked as follows:

They left England for New Zealand. *When* the Sandpiper was damaged by a sperm whale, they escaped onto a life raft *before* the boat sank. *First* they rowed towards the Galapagos islands. *Next/After that/Then* they attempted to get to the Central American coast *but* a hostile current dragged them back out to sea. They tried to attract the attention of passing ships *but* they sailed by, unaware of the couple's situation. *Eventually* they returned to Britain.

You could suggest students check the order of events by listening to the tape again and using their notes for reference.

23 Expressing emotions

Remind students that emotional expressions such as *to our horror*, *to my dismay* etc make a narrative more dramatic and personal.

You could extend this exercise to discuss modifiers, e.g. *great, intense, serious, enormous* etc and the ways these collocate. For example, we say *to our great relief/astonishment* and *to our intense relief*, but not *to our intense astonishment*. Unfortunately, there are no hard and fast rules. Familiarity can be improved by wider reading and practice.

ANSWERS

1 … when, to my annoyance/disappointment
2 … yesterday, to our great relief/joy,
3 … when, to his alarm/concern,
4 … and, to my delight/amazement/astonishment,
5 … heard, to our sorrow,
6 … when, to my disappointment/annoyance,

TENSES: ANSWERS

1 past continuous, past simple, past perfect simple
2 all past simple
3 past continuous, past simple, past continuous
4 future in the past, past simple, past simple, past perfect simple
5 past simple, past simple, past perfect simple, past simple, past simple, past perfect simple
6 future in the past, past simple, past perfect simple

24 Dictionary work: Prefixes

This exercise is quite high level, so you could treat it as a good opportunity for dictionary practice.

THE PREFIX *MAL-*: ANSWERS

1 malnutrition
2 malignant
3 malfunctioning
4 malpractice
5 malevolent
6 malicious
7 a malingerer

THE PREFIX *COUNTER-*: ANSWERS

1 counterbalance
2 counterproductive
3 counterattack
4 counteract
5 counterpart
6 counterarguments

You could round off the exercise on prefixes by discussing some other examples and their meanings, e.g. *mis*calculate, *out*grow, *over*compensate, *inter*-city, *de*rail, *re*consider.

25 Revision of reported speech

Incorporating some reported speech adds variety and immediacy to a story. Many students will already be familiar with the rules. You could revise them by discussing the example from the dialogue and encouraging students to formulate the rules, e.g. tenses shift one tense back, many modals do not change, pronouns change to reflect who is being spoken about, infinitives do not change.

Remind students that *that* is often omitted in reported speech, especially after *say* and *tell* e.g. *She said (that) she wanted to be alone.*

26 Reporting verbs

You could elicit other examples of reporting verbs such as *accuse, deny, apologize, think, offer, advise, reply, encourage, agree, recommend, complain.*

PRACTICE

The lone yachtswoman is an intriguing example of single-mindedness and determination.

POSSIBLE ANSWERS

1 She declared/explained she was attempting to break the world record for sailing non-stop east to west the 'wrong way' around the world.
2 She admitted/confessed her worst fear was personal failure. She insisted she wasn't trying to prove herself by sailing alone around the world. She said she had always been involved in challenging projects.
3 She acknowledged she was doing it because she was hoping to beat the world record of 161 days.
4 She said she was taking food and drink to last her up to 200 days.

5 She revealed that the food included 500 dried meals, 150 apples, …
6 She confessed that when she was thousands of miles from shore, and if she was injured, then she would be scared.
7 She mentioned that she had been taught to stitch her own flesh in an emergency.
8 She said that if there was a crisis, as long as danger was not imminent, she thought the answer was to make a cup of tea and think about it.
9 She declared/revealed that she knew she could handle the boat and she would find out whether she had the strength to beat the world record.
10 She revealed that she was being sponsored on the trip by security firms and credit agencies.

You could elicit other examples of direct speech changing into reported speech and introduced by different reporting verbs, e.g.

'This hotel is badly heated.'
He complained that the hotel was badly heated.

INTERNATIONAL OVERVIEW

ANSWERS

1 Floods and high winds
2 Landslides and volcanoes

The statistical information about natural disasters could provide a good starting point for a discussion about a variety of topics of international concern. You could encourage students to speculate about the causes of natural disasters and ask '*Do people ever contribute to global problems by their actions, or do these things just happen?*' This could lead to an interesting discussion as to whether pollution is causing climate change, making some parts of the world hotter and drier or causing flooding in other areas, leading to the failure of harvests, homelessness, famine, destitution, and so on.

This type of topic often appears in the exam and you might like to ask students to research a mini-project, e.g. the greenhouse effect or earthquakes, for a class presentation.

Back from the dead

The text comes from a popular newspaper. It's aimed at pet lovers and is a typical example of a human interest story. Pets and their owners are a fascinating, culturally-loaded topic, so it will be interesting to see how your students react to the distress of the owner who lost his beloved pet on holiday.

The questions on the reading text culminate in a guided summary which gives extra practice in a difficult skill area, whilst reinforcing tense usage.

28 Pre-reading tasks

The first pre-reading exercise gives students practice in structuring a narrative. Losing something is a common, annoying experience and most students should be able to relate to it.

Predicting the content and speculating about style and audience are, as always, reliable methods of harnessing students' subconscious expectations of the sort of text they are going to read.

30 Vocabulary check

ANSWERS

1	stranded	7	heartbroken
2	plunge	8	forlornly
3	spotted	9	bitch
4	pampered	10	tumbled
5	quarry	11	jagged
6	plummeted	12	sheer

31 True/false comprehension

ANSWERS

1F 2F 3T 4F 5T 6F 7F 8T 9F 10T

32 Narrative structure

Although IGCSE students are not expected to display great sophistication or ingenuity in shaping a narrative, this exercise will increase students' awareness of possible starting points in a story. It will also help them become more aware of the shifts in viewpoint and time which are typical of longer and more detailed newspaper reports.

All the points given in the Student's Book are possible reasons for telling the story in that particular style.

33 Writing a summary from notes

ANSWER

Mike Holden was on holiday in Cornwall. On the second day he went out for a walk with his dog, Judy. Judy started chasing a sheep. Unfortunately she was not used to the countryside and she fell over a cliff towards the sea. Her owner contacted the coastguard and a rescue team abseiled down the cliff. However, Judy could not be found and her owner returned to his home feeling very distressed. Two weeks later, a man rang. He said a birdwatcher had noticed Judy on a rock. A student had rescued her. She was thin but well. The vet said Judy had probably survived by drinking fresh water and feeding on a dead sheep.

34 Vocabulary: Adjectives

ANSWERS

ecstatic, happy, pleased, satisfied, indifferent, irritated, miserable, heartbroken

obese, fat, overweight, plump, slim, skinny, scrawny, emaciated

worshipped, pampered, well cared-for, ignored, neglected, abused

You could ask students to use these items in sentences of their own – as a homework exercise, for example.

35 Homonyms

Homonyms are, of course, very common in English. *Train*, for example has different meanings depending on whether it is a noun or a verb. This is an area of language learning which often puzzles students, so it can be worth making comparisons with other languages the students share.

ANSWERS

2 *Spotted* is an adjective meaning 'with a pattern of spots'.
3 *Sheer* in *sheer madness* is an intensifier meaning 'absolute'.

PRACTICE: ANSWERS

1 mine: noun, verb, or pronoun
2 sound: noun, verb, or adjective
3 stamp: noun or verb
4 dash: noun or verb
5 file: noun or verb
6 book: noun or verb
7 light: noun, verb or adjective
8 match: noun or verb

36 Revision of defining relative clauses

The aim of this and the following exercise is to revise the difference between defining and non-defining clauses and to help those students who, even at IGCSE level, are still writing mainly in simple sentences to vary their style of writing. IGCSE candidates whose sentences demonstrate variety in length and complexity as well as accuracy will receive very high marks. Using defining and non-defining clauses accurately is one way to do this.

PRACTICE: POSSIBLE ANSWERS

1 They prefer stories *which have* happy endings
2 The man *who lost his* dog on holiday has gone home without her.
3 The student *who survived the plane crash* received an award for bravery.
4 The watersport *I learned* on holiday has become my hobby.
5 The owner of the dog *which fell off the* cliff was distraught.
6 The man *whose dog fell off the* cliff was convinced his pet was dead.

37 Revision of non-defining relative clauses

PRACTICE: POSSIBLE ANSWERS

Students could treat this exercise as a problem-solving one and work together to come up with the extra information for each sentence.

1   Rahmia Altat, *who gave up her job last year*, now does voluntary work.
2   We heard about the heroic acts of the rescue workers, *which impressed us all*.
3   Nurse Thompson, *who attended the meeting specially*, demonstrated the life-saving techniques.
4   Drowning, *which is a common cause of death in children*, can usually be prevented.
5   Smoke alarms, *which are quite cheap*, should be fitted in every home.
6   My cousin Gina, *whose parents died when she was a baby*, is being brought up by her grandparents.
7   Mrs Nazir, *who had never entered a competition before*, won a trip to the Caribbean.
8   Edward Smith, *who had no children*, left his fortune to the dogs' home.
9   Our sailing teacher took us to an island, *where we had a picnic lunch*.

38 Functions quiz: Consoling and commiserating

Students should enjoy doing this quiz, which is quite lighthearted in feel. It provides more practice in choosing appropriate responses to sensitive situations. IGCSE students can find it hard to get the balance of sympathy right, with rather comic effects!

POSSIBLE ANSWERS

1   a or e
2   a or c
3   a
4   a, b or c
5   I'm sorry, you must be really disappointed.
6   Are you? Why? It looks all right to me.
7   Oh no! How terrible.

The expression '*Oh dear!*' is a useful sympathetic response in many situations and is heavily used by English people.

39 Spelling and pronunciation: The suffix –tion or –ion

 This exercise will boost students' awareness of the sound and spelling pattern of this suffix, pronounced /ʃn/.

After practising the pronunciation, students should mark the main stress in each word. Marking the stress, as always, helps develop listening and pronunciation skills.

ANSWERS

1   re'vision
2   'fashion
3   occu'pation
4   demon'stration
5   'passion
6   in'vention
7   qualifi'cation
8   defi'nition
9   recog'nition
10 ig'nition
11 exhi'bition
12 pro'motion

TAPESCRIPT

As in the Student's Book.

The matching exercise will ensure that the meanings of each word have been understood properly. As it's not too difficult, students should enjoy a feeling of achievement without undue effort!

ANSWERS

a	qualification	f	definition
b	occupation	g	promotion
c	invention	h	ignition
d	passion	i	recognition
e	exhibition	j	fashion

To round off the exercise, you could elicit more examples of words ending in *-ion*, e.g. *inspiration, comprehension, expression, attention*.

40 Language study: Adverbs

Students often make spelling mistakes when forming adverbs because they overgeneralise about the *-ly* ending and don't make the adjustments that are necessary to take account of the spelling of the adjective. The rules aren't complex, however, and mastering them needn't take long.

After the brief 'refresher' course in the functions of adverbs, students can go straight into the basic spelling rules for adding suffixes. Or you could adopt a problem-solving approach by giving them some examples and asking them to look for meaningful regularities in the spelling changes.

Examples:

comfortable	– *We sat comfortably.*
incredible	– *We were incredibly lucky.*
guilty	– *'I haven't taken anything,' said the thief guiltily.*
merry	– *She laughed merrily.*
rhythmic	– *They danced rhythmically.*
terrific	– *It was terrifically expensive.*

CAREERS AT SEA

Your students may like pondering over the career possibilities offered at sea. An interesting discussion could explore the pros and cons of living on a ship for long periods, raising issues of: family separation, being on call at all hours for emergencies, little privacy, cramped living conditions, coping with the discomfort of living on a ship in storms and gales etc. On the other hand, the basic needs of everyday life are provided for you (food, accommodation, leisure facilities, uniform etc), there's opportunity to travel, friendship and opportunities to develop your potential within a wide range of interesting occupations on offer. You could also explore the distinction between civilian and military vessels, and discuss which sort of ship would be preferable to work on, and why.

ANSWERS

surprisingly	necessarily
possibly	directly
definitely	quickly
lazily	normally

electronically	dramatically
daily	accordingly
immediately	heavily
ably	temporarily
hygienically	technically
healthily	suitably
economically	preferably
usually	capably
fully	efficiently
properly	happily
totally	responsibly
appropriately	frantically

41 Look, say, cover, write, check

The spelling list will, as always, help students recognise spelling sounds and patterns by developing visual awareness.

Reacting to the unexpected

42 Pre-reading task: Making notes

This next phase of exercises pulls together the skills students have been building up and gets them actually producing narratives. They start by making notes on something which happened to them. Encourage them to keep their notes and ask them to write up the ideas for homework.

It's interesting to follow up the note-making by discussing the implications of being involved in an unexpected experience.

43 Reading a model narrative

The model narrative shows, as always, the style and format students should aim for in their writing for the exam.

COMPREHENSION CHECK: ANSWERS

1   She was watching the children on the beach paddling and throwing pebbles.
2   No
3   Mouth to mouth resuscitation
4   They telephoned.
5   Learn to swim and take care near water.

44 Analysing the narrative

Remind students that their narratives need to be properly paragraphed. Many IGCSE students still produce blocks of text in the exam.

45 Dramatic expressions

Dramatic expressions make a narrative a little more sophisticated and increase its pace. Encourage students to use them. You could elicit similar ones, e.g. *I was thunderstruck*, *quick as a flash*, *in the nick of time*, and show how they could be used.

ANSWERS
1   E
2   A, B, C or D
3   B, C or D
4   A, B, C or D
5   F
6   A

Students could read their own sentences out loud.

46 Pre-writing discussion

Make sure students understand what a windsurfer does and what the sport is all about, especially if they have little experience of watersports.

47 Ways of developing an outline

The bare bones of a story about a windsurfer who is carried out to sea when strong winds blow up are provided. This gives students a basic plot to work from so they can concentrate on structuring the story well and providing interesting background details.

48 Building a story from a dialogue

Students write a narrative based on a conversation about an incident on a school trip to the seaside. The teacher lost her purse and one of the children helped her look for it. Students may not immediately see how they can produce a composition from a conversation, so it's useful to clarify how they can transfer the information revealed in the dialogue into a story told from Thomas's point of view.

Discuss with them how to shape the narrative and how to change the pronouns etc before they plunge in. Using some direct and reported speech would add interest and variety to their stories.

WIDER PRACTICE

1   The sea is a fascinating topic and students may enjoy researching many of its other aspects, e.g. its living creatures. If appropriate, cross-curricular links may be made with other subjects students are studying, e.g. geography, science.

2   Students can extend their story-telling skills by choosing a current news topic which absorbs them and tracing its development over several days. This could then be presented to the class.

3   In his book *The Kingdom by the Sea*, Paul Theroux travels the coastline of Britain and provides a witty but unflattering portrait of the people and their way of life. Students may enjoy hearing a few sections read aloud. Or they may enjoy hearing verses from Coleridge's narrative poem 'The Ancient Mariner' and exploring the idea of the sea symbolising a spiritual quest.

The Animal World

OVERVIEW

The main aim of the unit is further to develop students' ability to express reasoned opinions and arguments. Unit 4, Transport Issues, focused on presenting 'for and against' arguments. This unit looks at a wider variety of arguments within the topic of animals.

Sometimes exam questions ask students to present views and opinions explaining how or why a thing could happen. For example, in a discussion on endangered species, rather than being asked to take a stand for or against a proposal to help endangered species, students could be asked to express their opinions in a more measured way, e.g. 'Why do endangered species need our help and how can we ensure their protection?'

THEME

Students consider a number of questions on the theme of animals, including:

- How can zoos be more animal friendly?

- How can medical understanding and health standards be improved without our resorting to experiments on animals?

- How can we ensure working animals are treated fairly?

The items include a magazine article about animal experiments, a talk about a virtual reality zoo, and a leaflet about 'adopting' zoo animals.

LANGUAGE WORK

The language work further develops the skills needed to present a convincing argument. These include opinion language, rhetorical questions, and ways of adding emphasis. There is a range of vocabulary enlargement exercises related to animals. Spelling and pronunciation work focuses on plurals, and students practise the functions of disagreeing informally and expressing disappointment.

A fresh look at zoos

1 Animal vocabulary

The unit starts with some vocabulary input to familiarise students with key concept vocabulary for much of the unit. It's a good idea for them to work in pairs for exercises 1 and 2.

ANSWERS

A penguins
B monkey
C lion
D crocodile
E frog
F leopard
G lizard

mammals: rhino, monkey, gorilla, camel, kangaroo, leopard, elephant, goat, lion, dolphin, bear, wolf
reptiles: lizard, crocodile
fish: shark, salmon
birds: owl, penguin, eagle, parrot

Note: A frog is an *amphibian* and does not belong to any of the above categories.

2 Definitions

ANSWERS

1b **2**a **3**c **4**a **5**b

3 Pre-reading discussion

Allow the discussion about zoos to be as open as possible so that students have a real chance to think through the issues for themselves.

(The bird in the photograph is a *toucan*.)

4 Reading a model school magazine article

Encourage students to underline the opinion language as they read.

5 Comprehension check

ANSWERS

1 Because their teacher wanted them to see a modern zoo.
2 Very positive – he thought the animals seemed happy.
3 The origins and habits of the animals

4 They protect animals from predators, provide a caring environment, and educate people about wildlife.

5 Bad points about zoos to elicit could be:

Wild animals find conditions cramped, they lack space and privacy, and they are herded together when some animals are naturally solitary.

Animals are frustrated because they can't get enough exercise or respond to hunting instincts.

They become indolent as they have no need to search for food.

They suffer by having to live in unnatural climatic conditions.

Zoos are unnecessary – we can see animals in their natural habitat by watching wildlife programmes on TV.

6 Analysing the article
ANSWERS

A The opening paragraph is effective because it explains the background to the zoo visit. It shows audience awareness because it provides typical school details.

B Paragraph 2 questions attitudes to zoos with phrases such as *'I was pleasantly surprised by what I found'*, *'people said that zoos are full of smelly cages … Metro Park Zoo, however,'* and *'In my opinion'*.

C The phrase expressing disagreement is *'nothing could be further from the truth'*.

D *'I wasn't sure about the rights and wrongs of zoos'* tells us he has thought about both sides of the argument. *'On balance I feel that'* sums up his view of zoos and pulls the contrasting ideas together.

E The final paragraph ties together the whole structure effectively. It shows audience awareness by including a reference to his classmates.

7 Typical opinion language
ANSWERS

Opinion language used by Michael:

I just wasn't sure
As I see it, nothing could be further from the truth
On balance I feel that
to my mind
I think

Other possible opinion language:

In my view
Let's put it this way
I believe
If you ask me
As far as I'm concerned
As far as I can see

DISAGREEING WITH OTHER PEOPLE'S VIEWS: ANSWERS:

Students should tick:

Some people accuse them of … but nothing could be further from the truth.

Many people say that … . However, …

8 Making your mind up
ANSWERS

Michael used the phrase:
On balance I feel that

9 Writing a paragraph
You may like to let students work individually, or you may want to group together those working on the same topic to brainstorm some ideas before they write their paragraphs.

10 Reading aloud
Reading aloud provides a good opportunity to compare and contrast language structures and content. If you prefer, this could be done in groups rather than as a whole-class activity.

11 Expressions of contrasting meaning
Before students plunge into the exercise, it's worth pointing out that there is more than one possible answer each time. For example, *a bare, cramped room* could be contrasted with *a well furnished, gracefully-proportioned room.* The main aim of the exercise is for students to explore different possibilities and then choose the one that seems best to convey a contrasting meaning. At the end of the exercise, it's nice if they can share their answers and you can discuss different shades of meaning.

POSSIBLE ANSWERS

1 lively/interesting, informative lesson
2 a well-polished/shiny, smart pair of shoes
3 a contented/happy, healthy child
4 a well-cooked, tasty/delicious meal
5 a graceful, poised/flowing dance
6 a tidy/neat, well-maintained garden
7 attractive, easy-to-read/clear handwriting
8 a gleaming bicycle in perfect condition
9 a peaceful/calm, friendly/tolerant person
10 a soft, comfortable bed

12 Before you listen
The electronic zoo is a zoo which is planned for the future. It uses a range of sophisticated technologies to provide the visitor with a multi-media experience. Some very small live animals will be kept, but all the larger animals will be viewed on high-quality screens. There will be sound and climatic effects. The speaker stresses the educational aspects of the zoo.

You may wish to prepare students by asking what electronic means and elicit the fact that it is the basis of TV, videos, etc.

Tell students a little about the zoo without pre-empting the subsequent comprehension. For example, you could say '*Visitors will get the impression they are actually visiting the natural habitat of the wild animal – you will really feel as if you are in an African national park or in a tropical rainforest seeing and listening to the birds that live there.*' Students are likely to be fascinated by the concept, which is very futuristic in feel.

Possible questions for students to write could be:

How will the effect of actually visiting the natural habitat of an animal be created?

Why is it better than an ordinary zoo?

Are there any live animals?

What kind of information can visitors get about the origin and habits of the animals?

How will we know about the sounds animals make?

Will the zoo be very expensive to visit?

Where did the idea come from?

13 Vocabulary check

ANSWERS

audio-visual: involving sound as well as things to look at
filmed on location: filmed in real places, not in a studio or film set
live exhibits: real animals on display
natural history: the study of plants and animals

14 Listening for gist

 The speaker gives a lot of quite dense information, so you may want to let students listen more than once and pause the tape at intervals. Students need to be prepared for quite difficult talks for the listening part of the exam. This is an example of a more challenging monologue.

TAPESCRIPT

Now listen to the radio talk. Does the speaker answer your questions about electronic zoos?

PRESENTER: I'm delighted to introduce our next guest, David Wallace from Christopher Parsons Productions, who is going to talk to you about an interesting new development in zoos.
DAVID: Thank you, Sarah. It's a pleasure to be on the programme to discuss the spectacular new concept called the 'electronic zoo'. The zoo is very different from conventional zoos in that it aims to give a much broader impression of the life of many kinds of animals. It's going to do this by using the most advanced photographic and electronic techniques to reveal nature in a completely new way.
P: Oh, I say! That sounds really interesting!
D: The electronic zoo is a unique concept because, although no actual live large animals will be kept, the latest audio-visual technology will enable

visitors to learn far more about the habitat and behaviour of large animals. It also overcomes the accusation people make about zoos – that it's unfair to keep large animals in captivity. The concept of 'magic windows', for example, uses three large TV screens and six soundtracks. Wildlife will be filmed on location in its natural habitat, and the most interesting and varied behaviour will be used for the zoo. Visitors using 'magic windows' will have the illusion of being in, for example, a penguin colony or an Alaskan river where the bears are fishing for salmon. People won't feel they are passively watching a film or a video show. They'll have the sense of observing behaviour in 'real time' – I mean, animal behaviour exactly as it occurred during the filming.
P: How wonderful!
D: There will also be behavioural film from the world's best natural history libraries. This will avoid the disappointment visitors often feel because the animals they came to see are asleep.
P: Oh yes, that's often happened to me.
D: There'll be interactive videos, too – you can slow down or replay the animals' actions on screen by pressing a button. The electronic zoo will also have a wide range of live animal exhibits, and these will be small species: small fish, reptiles, birds and insects. You could say the natural world will be represented in a more comprehensive way than conventional zoos, since ninety-five per cent of all animals in the world are smaller than the size of a hen's egg.
P: Hmm! Yes, I suppose they are, when you come to think of it.
D: One of the special characteristics of the electronic zoo will be the use of natural sounds. The most dramatic and beautiful sounds animals make in their own habitat will be reproduced using CD and computers. And there'll be artificial grass, bushes and so on, to create the atmosphere you would find in the natural world.
P: I'm sorry, David, it sounds absolutely marvellous, but I have to interrupt you there as we're running out of time. If you'd like to know more …

15 True/false comprehension

ANSWERS

1 true **2** false **3** false **4** false **5** false **6** false

16 Post-listening discussion

The talk may arouse a lot of interest in the impact technology will have in the world of the future. You may like to ask students what would be better and worse about a future where it becomes easier and easier to simulate experience, and where 'virtual reality' becomes the norm.

The target group of the electronic zoo is really anybody who is interested in finding out more about animals, particularly those who feel at ease with recent technologies.

17 Functions

 Encourage students to express their views on the appropriacy of using large animals in the circus.

Silvia's voice goes down as she expresses disappointment. You could present a model of a disappointed tone, e.g. '*I was looking forward to*

seeing (name a person students will be familiar with from TV) at the theatre in real life, but she didn't give a good performance.' You could ask students to relate their own experiences of disappointment arising from unfulfilled expectations, such as a boring film, meal or party.

Adjectives and comparative structures are important in this exercise so you may like to revise the *not as … as …* form (which can be tricky), with the relevant adjectives (*spectacular, superb, fascinating, delightful, enchanting*, etc) for description.

You may like to ask pairs of students to take the parts of Malik and Silvia and read the dialogue aloud. Students usually like doing this, and you can ask the rest of the class to decide how disappointed 'Silvia' manages to sound.

TAPESCRIPT

As in the Student's Book.

EXPRESSING DISAPPOINTMENT ETC

You could ask students to tick any expressions they recognise from the dialogue.

18 Practice dialogues

Students progress from the prompted dialogue to making up their own conversations.

You may like to round off the exercise by introducing the colloquial word *hype,* meaning an activity intended to raise expectations, as in *'There was so much hype about the electronic zoo but when I went it was a let-down.'*

Animal experimentation

19 Pre-reading discussion

The following sequence of exercises focuses on the rights and wrongs of animal experimentation. The magazine article puts forward a highly positive view of the issues, and students then go on to explore why this may or may not be a complete picture of all that animal experimentation involves. It's a difficult text, so students do a variety of tasks to prepare them for it, intellectually and linguistically.

After students have commented on the photograph, you could raise the question of using animals for dissection in science lessons (if their studies involve this) and ask them how they feel about it. You could ask if they have had immunisation, and say that the vaccination against polio, for example, was discovered through animal experimentation.

ETHICAL QUESTIONS

Make sure students have understood the concept of ethics before they go on to discuss the ethical

questions in pairs or small groups. Ethical questions will be central to later discussions on the treatment of animals, but they are very culturally based. What is 'ethical' in one culture isn't necessarily seen as right in another. You could check this by asking about wider issues that students may have a view on. It might be nicest to choose examples that relate directly to students' culture.

Other ideas are:

Should a couple of over 60 years be allowed to adopt a baby?

Is it right to keep people who have almost no chance of recovery alive for years on life support machines?

Should terminally ill people be allowed to end their own lives?

Finally, students are asked what they think about animal experiments, after having had a chance to review the various ethical issues. They are offered some further useful vocabulary for giving opinions.

20 Predicting content

ANSWER

As the writer is a campaigner for medical experiments on animals, the arguments are likely to be rather extreme.

21 Vocabulary check

ANSWERS

An *emotive* issue is one which arouses strong feelings.

A *controversial* issue is one about which people disagree strongly.

22 Reading for detail

Students can't take good notes from a text they haven't understood. The questions aim to check understanding before going on to the more challenging note-taking exercise. You will need to allow enough time for students to read the text in detail.

ANSWERS

1   Research using animals
2   The discovery that blood circulates through our veins, knowledge of the way the lungs work, the discovery of vitamins and hormones
3   Animals are given human diseases so that researchers can study their reactions.
4   Researchers want to prevent suffering but they may have to cause animal suffering to do so.
5   They might help animals by finding a cure for animal illnesses.

23 Vocabulary

ANSWERS

1F   **2**E   **3**C   **4**B   **5**A   **6**D

24 Post-reading discussion

It will be fascinating to hear students' views after they have studied a very persuasive argument in favour of experiments on animals.

25 Note-taking

Before students begin the bullet points (which are a popular format for note-taking in the exam), it would be useful to draw attention to three key words in the exercise: *reasons*, *achievements* and *steps*.

ANSWERS

- The experiments aim to find cures and treatment for human illnesses.

Achieved so far:

- advances in medical understanding
- advances in the practical applications of medicine

Humane approaches:

- reduce the number of animals in each experiment
- replace animals with alternatives where possible
- refine experiments so they cause the least possible harm to animals

26 How the writer achieves his effects

A   The aim of this exercise is to study devices the writer uses to achieve a dispassionate style. You could ask *'Does the writer seem aggressive and angry about medical experiments being the right thing to do?'* Questions along these lines will help students become more analytical about the artifice the writer is using.

This, and the subsequent exercises, would be challenging even for native speakers, so there are a number of prompts in the Student's Book to help students think along the right lines.

B   Students should find the checklist helpful in exploring the devices the writer uses. *'He makes us laugh at people who campaign against medical experiments'* is incorrect. Being 'fair' to the views of people who are against his work is one of the ways he appears objective.

Examples in the text of these points are:

He suggests animals are well cared for by saying *'The worst these animals have to put up with is living in a cage with regular food and water …'* (*line 81*).

Statistics are given on the numbers of people affected by polio, the numbers of animals used for experiments, and the numbers of dogs dying of distemper.

Factual information is given about advances in medical understanding, medical treatment for diseases, and advances in surgery.

A reassuring, caring image of researchers is put across by saying *'People who experiment on animals are just the same as the rest of us'* (*line 117*) and *'because we like animals'* (*line 121*).

He seems to try to understand the point of view of his opponents by admitting that the animal experiments cause suffering: *'The golden rule of laboratory animal welfare is to minimise any distress involved'* (*line 86*).

You could also ask:

'Does he use a lot of emotive, upsetting language?' (No, the opposite is true.)

'Does he quote from famous authorities?' (No, although this is a common technique used for adding weight to an argument.)

27 The angle of the argument

This is a good opportunity to contrast the notion of a 'for and against' approach to an argument with the 'how' approach, which requires reasoning and explanation from different standpoints. To give another example, you could ask *'Are you more likely to be asked for your opinions for or against reducing road accidents, or for your opinions as to how they might be reduced?'*

28 Understanding bias in an argument

A   The aim of this exercise it to show how the impression of objectivity can be reduced when we consider how much the writer has left out of his argument. Students try to find points against medical experiments on animals in order to establish a more complete and rounded picture of the issues. 'Points against' is a slight oversimplification: what students are doing, in fact, is considering a wider variety of aspects of the issue.

B   Each point is quite condensed, so it's worth taking each one in turn and making sure students understand what is being said.

You could round off the work on understanding bias by asking students to sum up how fair they feel the writer is to the topic, now that they have had a chance to consider more aspects of the issue.

29 Writing an article for the school newsletter

Students are asked to transfer their understanding of medical experiments on animals and the language used for opinion and persuasion to writing a school newsletter article. The question is intellectually quite challenging and has a different slant from the 'for and against' compositions they have written before.

Make sure students understand that they are writing a measured argument. They can show this by using such contrast expressions as *whilst*, *although*, *even though*, e.g. *Whilst animal experiments have led to important medical advances, there are other ways in which health care can progress.*

Key points to include could be: the limitations of medical experiments (animals react to drugs and experiments in a different way from humans); the alternatives to research on animals (e.g. more tests on human volunteers which can be more reliable, the use of medical technology such as lasers and ultrasound techniques); preventive measures to reduce human illness (e.g. better health education, the provision of clean water supplies).

Allow students enough time to ask any questions and to write the composition, as they are likely to find it a demanding task. Remind them of the need to use a firm closing paragraph. The main idea to convey is that there are alternatives.

30 Prepositions after verbs

It is always useful to practise prepositions with students of all levels. Total (or near total) accuracy with prepositions takes a long time to master.

Other examples to elicit are:

I can only *guess at* his whereabouts.
Animals *differ* in many ways *from* people.
I want to *complain* to the manager *about* their attitude.

PRACTICE: ANSWERS

1 experiment on
2 bother about, dying from/of
3 surprised at
4 object to
5 contribute to
6 quarrel with
7 depend on
8 died of
9 provide him with
10 respond well to

Some other verbs followed by the prepositions in the exercise are as follows:

worry/gossip/think/speculate/argue *about*
look/wonder/hint/smile/throw *at*
hear/depart/benefit *from*
accuse/remind/dream *of*
concentrate/bet/rely/congratulate/agree *on*
listen/dedicate/appeal *to*
collaborate/sympathise/help/agree *with*

31 Spelling and pronunciation: Regular plurals

However familiar students are with plurals, they still present problems and are at the root of many spelling mistakes and pronunciation difficulties.

Ask students to read the list of nouns silently and to double check the meanings of more tricky words, e.g. *wasps, spiders*.

 Students now listen to the 16 words listed and identify the pronunciation of each ending. The words are spoken twice.

ANSWERS

/s/: cats, insects, wasps, goats
/z/: hens, dogs, spiders, birds, cows, bees
/iz/: cages, faces, horses, houses, monkeys, roses

TAPESCRIPT

As in the Student's Book.

32 Spelling and pronunciation: Irregular plurals

Ask students to practise the pronunciation of the irregular plurals. Other examples to elicit could be:

-*es*: branches, watches, wishes

-*ves*: selves, wives, thieves, shelves, halves, lives, loaves (A common exception is *roofs*.)

Change in the vowel: *foot – feet*

-*es*: heroes

-*ies*: babies, families

33 Vocabulary
ANSWERS

1 sheep, lambs
2 bears, wolves, wildcats
3 deer, geese, foxes
4 mice
5 crocodiles, rhinos, teeth
6 caterpillars, butterflies

34 Look, say, cover, write, check

The word list recycles vocabulary students have met and helps them learn problematic words.

Animals in sport

35 Discussion

The following sequence of exercises explores the role of animals in sport. You could begin by asking students if they are involved with animals in any sport they do, e.g. horse riding. Ask them to describe what they enjoy about the activity and whether the animal enjoys it too.

Horse racing is popular in Britain and many other countries. You could ask whether training animals to perform under pressure and in public is unkind in any way, or whether it depends on how the animals are treated

Fieldsports or blood sports are much more controversial, and there are many groups actively campaigning either in their defence or against them. It will be interesting to hear students' views on such sports (and also to see if they modify their opinions later, after considering the letter in exercise 37).

36 Fieldsports: People's opinions

Asking students to put a tick or cross will help them focus on what they are reading. The sentence structures contain examples of emphatic forms which they will be studying in more detail in later exercises.

37 Letter completion: My views on foxhunting

Students often approach this kind of cloze exercise blissfully unaware of the pitfalls it conceals! You may need to explain the subtleties of the choices which might confuse some students.

ANSWERS

1 I think
2 cruel
3 claims
4 Frankly
5 an innocent
6 Contrary to popular belief
7 Furthermore
8 As I see it
9 but
10 disgusting

38 Vocabulary: Words for feelings

You may wish to recommend that students use dictionaries for this exercise, as the level is fairly demanding.

ANSWERS

1 sickened
2 anxious
3 contemptible
4 thrilled
5 penitent
6 preposterous
7 compassionate
8 tearful

You could ask students to use some of this vocabulary in sentences of their own in order to help retention.

39 Language study: Adding extra emphasis

There are many different ways to express emphasis in writing. The structures in this exercise have been selected as some of the most accessible and straightforward to learn, so hopefully students will be confident in using them in their freer writing later.

You may like to ask students to read the sentences aloud to show the emphasis through the intonation pattern. You could discuss the fact that in speech

we are less reliant on changes in structure to show emphasis, as we have the chance to change our tone of voice.

ANSWERS

Emphatic forms in exercise 36 are:

What makes me sick is, the people who object, I do think, What I most enjoy, The places where I shoot, What makes me cross is people who …

40 Practice

ANSWERS

1 What she admires is/are attempts to alleviate animal suffering.
2 What we need is/are better fences to stop animals wandering onto the road.
3 What the safari park wardens worry about is animals escaping.
4 The place where you can see owls, eagles and hawks is a falconry centre.
5 What we didn't understand is/was that animals are adapted to live in certain habitats.
6 What I didn't realise is/was how animals depend on each other.
7 The people who are responsible for the reduction in rhino numbers are hunters.
8 The place where the golden eagle prefers to nest is in treeless, mountainous country.
9 What ought to concern us is/are endangered species in our own country.
10 What I want is the right to object to things I think are wrong.

41 More practice

ANSWERS

1 Having a pet has made her so happy.
2 We all shouted, 'Do tell us more about your adventures.'
3 Do take lots of photos when you visit the wildlife park.
4 I never realised that baby rhinos were so affectionate.
5 Raising orphaned wildlife is so worthwhile.
6 Your cat does enjoy his milk, doesn't he?
7 You do look tired/You look so tired today.
8 Caged animals are so miserable.
9 Gordon felt so sorry/did feel sorry for the animals he saw at the circus.
10 I do worry about, you know.
11 Do help yourself to some more cake.
12 Do come in, Sophie. I'm so pleased to see you.

42 Comparing languages

It will be interesting to hear students describe how they add emphasis in their own language(s).

43 Writing sentences

Encourage students to write a few sentences of their own using emphatic forms.

Animals at work

44 Thinking about working animals

The following sequence of exercises considers the role of animals which are kept by people to generate income. The discussion points centre on the responsibilities people have towards their animals, and what can be done about cruelty to working animals. Students also consider whether intensive farming is ethical.

A Ask students to look at the pictures of animals and elicit ideas about what animals are used for in their country(ies).

B Other responsibilities owners have towards animals could include: giving them water, sheltering them, keeping them in a reasonably clean and comfortable condition, making sure they get enough rest and exercise, getting a vet for them if they are ill.

45 Discussing ethical issues

Students may have strong opinions about whether animals are overworked or treated harshly by their owners. Encourage them to be specific about any problems they may have observed, as this helps them think through their ideas more analytically.

You could extend the discussion to consider the use of animals to help people in difficulty (rescue dogs, dogs for the blind, etc) or to detect criminals (police dogs, guard dogs). Such dogs often have a high level of intelligence and training. Exploring more about how they can help humans fight crime or save lives might be a nice follow-up.

46 Building a letter from prompts

MODEL ANSWER

Dear Sir,

I am writing in response to recent articles saying that people who keep animals for profit are 'cruel and heartless'. My family make a living from keeping sheep. In my view, our life is harder than the animals'!

In lambing time, for example, there is no day off and no rest. My father gets up as soon as it is light and hurries out to the first task of the day without even bothering to have a drink. He works for several hours without a break. He checks the lambs that were born in the night or attends ewes that are having difficulty giving birth. He brings sickly lambs indoors to be bottle-fed.

He tries to get round the flock four or five times a day, often in driving snow or cruel winds. If there is a specific problem, he has to go out several times a night with a flash light. Although expensive, the vet is always called when he is needed.

It is true that every ewe or lamb that dies is a financial loss to us, so it is in our own interest to care for the sheep. The sheep are eventually sold at the market. How could/can we live any other way? But we are certainly not the 'ruthless exploiters' of your article. In fact, nothing could be further from the truth.

Yours faithfully,

Gillian Connor

47 Assessing the argument

Encourage students to re-read the letter when it is correct to get a sense of textual flow, as this is difficult to do when they are building up the letter from the prompts. You could ask a very able student who has a good command of intonation to read the letter aloud to the group, or you may prefer to do it yourself.

48 The closing paragraph

As always, ask students to pay particular attention to the end of the letter, which gives an opinion to round it off. Explain that this is appropriate for this type of composition, and compare it with how you might end a 'for and against' essay.

49 Vocabulary: Collective nouns

ANSWERS

1 cows, elephants, deer
2 sheep, goats
3 fish
4 dogs, wolves
5 bees, locusts, ants

Point out that *flock* is also the collective noun for birds.

You may like to extend this exercise by considering the names of the sounds animals and birds make (e.g. *buzz, bark, moo, roar, squawk, twitter*, which are onomatopoeic in English) or by eliciting the names of animal homes (*kennel, pen, stable, cage, nest, lair*, etc).

50 Discussion: Intensive farming

Intensive farming of animals may or not be familiar to students, so the discussion will need to be tailored to their experience. Pesticides are used on a more global scale, although very small farmers may not use them as much. Depending on their background, students may have positive views of intensive farming: because it uses more technology the results are more dependable, and it is labour-saving. They might feel it is kinder to farmers than traditional, back-breaking methods where whole crops are blighted through uncontrolled diseases, possibly leading to financial ruin. In any event, it will be stimulating to hear their ideas.

It would be useful to check students' understanding of the 'food chain' concept. They may be familiar with this from their science or biology lessons.

Reasons people may object to intensive farming (which is called *factory farming* by those who criticise it) usually centre on the conditions in which the animals etc are kept, e.g. hens and pigs may be kept in dark windowless sheds, with very little space to move around, and their feeding controlled automatically. People claim that animals kept in these conditions usually produce tasteless, tough meat, eggs and so on. There is also concern that livestock which are fed regular doses of hormones could pass these on to consumers in the food chain.

Students are asked to think of possible solutions to the objections people make about intensive farming. There are no easy answers, but solutions might include helping farmers financially to produce food on a smaller, more kindly scale, and giving subsidies to help them adopt organic methods and reduce the use of pesticides. Food companies could be obliged to give fuller information to the consumer through more comprehensive labelling of products.

51 Punctuation

It would be useful to revise students' grasp of the main points of punctuation before going into the exercise.

MODEL ANSWER

Dear Sir,

Like many of your readers, I want to buy healthy food which is produced in a way which is fair to farm workers and animals. Furthermore, I don't believe food production should damage the environment. Many farmers in our area say that it is cheaper to rear animals under intensive conditions than it is to give them a decent life. However, if farmers were given subsidies, they would be able to afford more space and comfort for animals. Farmers get subsidies for intensive methods, so why not pay them for a kinder approach?

Similarly, many of the farms around here use harmful pesticides which can get into the food chain. Farmers say it is less expensive to use pesticides than to use more natural or 'organic' methods, which require a bigger labour force and so would be more expensive. What is more expensive in the end – subsidies to the farmers for organic farming or a damaged environment? In my view, we have a right to know what is in our food. Tins, packets and fresh food should be labelled by food companies as 'free range' or 'factory farmed', or whether pesticides were used, so that we know exactly what we are eating.

I realise my ideas might lead to higher food prices, but I have no doubt at all it would be worth it.

Yours faithfully,

Shahar Rishani

52 Checking the text flow

Encourage students to read the letter again when they have corrected it, to get a sense of textual flow.

53 Further thoughts

It will be interesting to hear students' views on Shahar's arguments.

Some of the ways intensive production of food might be unfair to farm workers could include: low wages, long hours, and working in unsafe conditions (e.g. spraying pesticides, driving machinery) without adequate protection. Also, workers might feel 'dehumanised' by having to treat animals as units in a production line. You could tell students that supermarkets in some countries are now choosing to promote 'ethically produced food' to attract more customers, and as a way of demonstrating support for fair treatment of workers. It would be interesting to hear what they think of this development.

Caring for animals

54 Discussion

Many students are fond of animals and may have one or more pets at home, so this should be a lively discussion based on their own experience. You may like to tell them cats and dogs are the most popular pets in Britain.

People who keep animals as pets have the additional responsibility of giving them attention and affection. Some points to elicit as to why a pet isn't suitable for everyone could include:

They cost money to keep (for food and vets' bills).

It takes time to give them care and a regular routine.

Some animals have specific needs: dogs need exercising, ponies need a grazing area and must be fed, mucked out and exercised twice a day.

Large animals are unsuitable pets in small apartments or houses.

Cats and dogs like to spend time outside, so may need a secure garden.

Puppies and kittens need house training.

Many animals need companionship, and people who are away from home regularly can't give them this.

Certain breeds of dog are more suitable as working animals, than as family pets – especially where there are children.

Exotic pets, such as certain reptiles, fish and birds, may need special diets and/or living conditions.

55 Rhetorical questions

Using a rhetorical question device gives students' writing that extra touch of sophistication the exam is looking for.

It can be artificial to think of rhetorical questions out of context. However, when they have assimilated the pattern, students should be able to incorporate this device into their writing styles.

56 Restructuring statements into rhetorical questions

ANSWERS

1 Is a vegetarian meal always healthy?
2 Who can say the farmers are wrong?
3 Which is more important/better: to save an animal or (to) save someone's life?
4 Who knows the extent of the problem?
5 Do we really need all these fur coats and leather handbags/all the fur coats … we buy?
6 Wouldn't we all be happier knowing that our food was free of chemicals?
7 Isn't it about time we remembered endangered species at home?
8 Shouldn't we consider farm workers before worrying about animals?

Asking students to find examples in the letters they have corrected will reinforce learning. They should underline the following: *How could we live any other way?*, *why not pay them for a kinder approach?* and *What is more expensive in the end … environment?*

57 Vocabulary: Young animals

ANSWERS

1 cub
2 duckling
3 chick/chicken
4 calf
5 kitten
6 pup/puppy
7 kid
8 foal
9 calf
10 calf
11 cygnet
12 cub

58 Comparing languages

It will be interesting to hear expressions for young animals in students' own language(s).

Students have considered a lot of serious issues in the unit so far, so it might be fun to introduce some light-hearted diversion. You could ask what animal characteristic students would like to have for themselves. They could decide whether they would like to grow a woolly coat for cold days, have the strength of an ox, swim underwater like a fish or dolphin, have the grace of a wildcat or the speed of a jaguar, and so on.

59 Could you help animals?

This can be a very open and lively discussion covering a whole range of issues which have been raised in the unit. Try to encourage students to be specific and focus on practical ways they could support animals and wildlife. You could ask a student to write up a list of points from the discussion on the board.

INTERNATIONAL OVERVIEW

ANSWER

The blue whale has been most affected by whaling, according to the chart.

You may like to ask students to say what they know about these and other whales, or to find out more.

The *blue whale* is the largest animal on earth, measuring 31 metres and weighing over 100 tonnes. It feeds on plankton. The *sperm whale* is the largest of the toothed whales and was formerly hunted for the *spermaceti* in its head, an oil-like substance used in lubricants and cosmetics. The *killer whale* is a member of the dolphin family.

Whales are extremely intelligent creatures and have a sophisticated communication system.

(The photograph in the Student's Book shows a *beluga whale*.)

60 Reading for gist

As always, encourage students to try to work out the meaning of unfamiliar words from the context.

61 Reading comprehension

ANSWERS

1 Most animals are available for adoption.
2 It uses the money for breeding programmes to save animals from extinction.
3 An adoption certificate, regular copies of 'Zoo Update', and four free entry tickets.
4 To save a corridor of rainforest in Central America, as a haven for wildlife.
5 They are in Thailand, and they provide natural sanctuaries for Indo-Chinese tigers orphaned by poaching.

62 Building a newsletter article from a first draft

You may like to allow students to discuss the model answer and compare it with their own writing. It shows how material in the Student's Book can be used as a resource and combined with original writing.

MODEL ANSWER

We could help endangered species by adopting a zoo animal at our local zoo, King's Park. When we visit it on school trips we could check on its progress.

Adopting an animal means we would get a zoo newsletter describing the adoption programmes for endangered species. The zoo raises money through the adoption scheme for its breeding programmes. We could also get a personalised plaque on the animal's enclosure. Wouldn't that be great?

In addition to the adoption scheme, the zoo is running a Wild Action appeal to help support two projects. Rainforest Action Costa Rica is trying to save a corridor of tropical forest to provide a safe haven for wildlife. The second project, the Tiger Trust, is raising money for natural sanctuaries for tiger cubs in Thailand orphaned by poaching. There is an appalling trade in body parts and tiger bones. Isn't it terrible to think that only 5,000 tigers remain in the wild now?

A school survey found that many of us wanted to help animals threatened by extinction. Adopting a zoo animal or making a donation to the Wild Action Appeal will help – and we get tiger T-shirts too!

WIDER PRACTICE

1   Having studied animal rights in detail, it would be interesting for students to discuss the rights of people. This could be a fascinating and far-reaching topic, following on well from the work they have done on ethical questions and extending their personal and social education.

Students might enjoy working out their 'rights' which you could tailor for their particular situation. With rights come responsibilities. Defending 'responsibilities' is another stretching problem-solving exercise.

Some possible rights/responsibilities for young people could be:

- to have an education/to make the most of my educational opportunities
- to have my own opinions and views/to listen to the opinions of others and to try to understand their points of view
- to meet friends of my own age and join clubs/ to explain to concerned adults what they need to know about my friends and agree a time to come home
- to have access to medical care/to look after myself and to do what I can to stay in good health.

2   The topic of animals lends itself well to cross-curricular work. You could liaise with science and environmental teaches to discuss more about the food chain, ecology, etc.

3   There is a wealth of factual information available about animals themselves: animal families, origins, habits, breeding patterns. Students could find out about an animal they are interested in and present a stimulating factual talk to the group.

4   Video or audio taping a controversial discussion about farming or zoos, or animal management, could provide a basis for heated debate, as could inviting a speaker on the topic to class.

5   Supporting an animal or wildlife charity might be worth considering. Students would receive a lot of information, and it would give them a valuable sense of making a difference to some issues of global concern.

The World of Work

OVERVIEW

This unit consolidates the skills needed if students are to show 'evidence of verbal sophistication' and the ability to sustain quality in their writing, which are the criteria for gaining the highest examination marks.

This unit also introduces the comprehension and interpretation of statistical data, including graphs, bar charts, etc.

THEME

The theme of the unit is work. This is approached through developing more understanding of the skills and qualities needed for work, common problems faced in the workplace, and the way in which school prepares you for work. Students also discuss unemployment, with particular reference to school leavers, and strategies for increasing school and college leavers' chances of finding the job they want.

The issues raised are:

- How do surveys and the portrayal of teenagers in the media influence public opinion and adversely affect their chances of training or employment?

- How does stereotyping operate at work, and why might it be harmful?

- How does school promote maturity and responsibility for work?

- How can employment levels be increased (using examples and knowledge based on students' own countries)?

The texts include a factual article about the work involved in developing and producing a new item for the market – chocolate. There is also a chatty magazine article about the employment of people with disabilities. The listening exercise is an interview with a personnel officer working for a chain of electrical stores.

LANGUAGE WORK

The unit consolidates the functions and skills approach of the earlier units. New language work focuses on expressing figures and approximations, and criticising statistical information. Pronunciation focuses on linking sounds.

The rewards of work

1 Discussion

The introductory discussion focuses on why people work. The reasons are wide and varied. Encourage students to come up with ideas such as:

- to use skills and qualifications
- to have fun
- to travel
- to enjoy company benefits: car, health insurance, tax-free loans, etc
- for security
- to get out of the house
- for standing in the community
- to give routine and structure to the day
- to make a difference to society
- to raise their standard of living
- to have a break from domestic chores and commitments
- to express different aspects of their personality
- to get a sense of achievement
- to enjoy using specialised things only available at work
- to enjoy wearing special clothes/uniform.

You could also ask '*What is the effect on people when they lose their job?*'

This could elicit interesting ideas which can be developed later in the unit, when there is a focus on unemployment.

2 Skills and qualities for work

The matching exercise encourages students to focus on what is really essential for an occupation.

ANSWERS

1C 2J 3E 4I 5H 6G 7D 8F 9B 10A

3 Pre-reading tasks

A Students are going to read about how a new bar of chocolate is researched, developed, tested out on consumers and launched. You could introduce this topic by telling them briefly about a new type of product you have tried yourself, what you liked about it, why you tried it and whether you are going to go on using it.

B The text itself focuses on the challenges, in business terms, of making a new product successful. The exercise can be more fully exploited if you also highlight any business-related vocabulary students bring up while discussing the pre-reading question. Possible words might include: *consumer*, *market*, *lifestyle*, *competition*, *profits*, *sales*.

Challenges involved in making a new product successful which students may suggest are:

You have to know who is likely to buy it (the target group).

You have to understand how it will fit into the existing market for this type of product.

You have to have the financial resources to make the project feasible.

You have to work out a realistic figure for how much it will cost to make it.

You need an effective marketing strategy – TV, newspapers, magazines, hoardings, etc, so people know about it and are tempted to try it.

You have to be able to sustain the sales.

4 Predicting

The pictures accompanying the text are a useful resource, as they illustrate the processes described in the article. Encourage students to study them carefully.

5 Reading for gist

This text is quite long and the vocabulary level is quite high, so you may want to ask students to stop reading at the end of each section to check general comprehension. For example, at the end of the introductory section you could ask '*How much does someone in Britain spend on chocolate in a year?*'

6 Reading comprehension

ANSWERS

1   To try to identify opportunities for new products.
2   If not, it will quickly attract competition from competitors.
3   They want people's opinions on the taste of the chocolate, and the impact the advert had on them.
4   The smallest increase was in 1993.
5   The paragraph should include the following points:
      - too easy for rivals to copy
      - price not right, too expensive for the market
      - might not come out right in the production process (too soggy, etc)
      - might be difficult to make the taste consistent.

The following point could also be included, as it is implied:

      - might be taking too long to get the product right.

7 Post-reading discussion

Students may be very surprised at the amount of effort and money that goes into researching and developing a new product. It will be interesting to hear their reactions.

8 Vocabulary

Students can work in pairs to produce a lexical set for business. Monitor the exercise and encourage them to use dictionaries.

ANSWERS

producing, companies, manufacturer, brand, competition, machinery, investment, factory, produced economically, price-sensitive market, formula, production, price, products, projects, consumers, buy, mass-production, process of development

COLLOCATIONS

Suggest that students work together, using dictionaries, to come up with collocations for *stiff*, *sensitive* and *delicious*.

Point out that *stiff* in the text is used metaphorically to mean 'harsh' or 'difficult', but it can have a literal meaning, as in *stiff neck*. *Sensitive* in the text suggests something fragile or easily affected by outside pressures.

POSSIBLE ANSWERS

stiff: neck, drink, punishment, breeze, climb, interview, exam
sensitive: skin, eyes, instrument, person, animal, plant, relationship, topic/subject
delicious: drink, food, meal, scent/smell/perfume

As always, ask students to record new items in their vocabulary records, with an example of how words could be used.

9 A rewarding job

The aim of this exercise is to develop students' understanding of the variety of feelings people involved in the chocolate bar project might have, and to think about the skills and qualities they would need for their work.

POSSIBLE ANSWERS

feelings: elated, happy, satisfied, enthusiastic, interested, intrigued, disappointed, irritated, bored, despondent
skills and qualities: creativity, ability to work in a team, perseverance, attention to detail, ability to work on your own

10 Sharing ideas
POSSIBLE ANSWERS

Most of the reasons for working suggested for exercise 1 could apply here.

The skills and qualities mentioned in exercise 2 which are relevant are: patience, good communication skills, artistic flair, business acumen, imagination.

11 Understanding visual data

Students should be familiar with graphs, bar charts, etc from work in other areas of the curriculum. They may feel more confident with data that is presented in a visual form than with the language which describes the data. However, if they find comprehension of visual data very difficult, it's a good idea to let them have extra practice by bringing in supplementary material for homework or class use, before moving on with further work on interpretation. (The Wider Practice section at the end of this unit has examples of more visual data.)

Reassure students by explaining that comprehension and description of visual data is enough; they won't actually have to draw any charts etc of their own in the exam.

Ask students to re-read the opening paragraph of 'A bar is born'.

POSSIBLE ANSWER

Students should come up with an answer along the lines of:

'The two bar charts reflect the information in the first paragraph by showing that consumption of chocolate has grown and spending has increased. The first chart shows the amount spent each year. The second chart breaks down the spending on chocolate into weekly amounts per head of population. This is a different way of showing the information in the first paragraph, which gives figures for spending per person per year.'

12 Role play: Product development meeting

The role play enables students to act out the occupational roles which were suggested by the text. This is done through role-playing a meeting to discuss the feasibility of researching and developing a new chocolate bar. The role play includes a discussion of problems with the formula, technology, price, the target group, advertising strategies etc.

The aim is to enable students to activate as much passive knowledge as possible. However, it would be useful to revise the functions of interrupting, offering advice/suggestions/opinions and expressing disagreement, so students are well prepared. Tell students that the emphasis will be on fluency, spontaneity and activating passive knowledge.

Students should do the role play in groups of four. Let them have some time to quietly read and absorb their role information individually, and check any problems with comprehension. Alternatively, you could draw together all the people with the same role for a joint briefing. Make sure they understand what is expected of them, and clarify any misunderstandings before they begin.

Facts and figures

13 Approximations

ANSWERS

The stress in *per cent* falls on *cent*.
1H 2C 3B 4A 5F 6D 7E 8G

Elicit from students the idea that approximations are used to make bald statistics more understandable, by comparing them to amounts that the general public find easy to imagine.

The disadvantage might be that approximations can be used to slant information so that it creates a positive or negative impression. It is not, strictly speaking, a disadvantage, but simply something for students to be aware of.

14 Questioning statistics

A   The aim of this exercise is to develop students' ability to criticise authoritative-sounding statistics.

B   The answers to the questions might reveal that the survey was carried out by a market research company on behalf of a political pressure group which is opposed to working mothers and wants to influence public opinion against them. The size of the sample might reveal that it was too small to be meaningful. The questions could be loaded or too vague – 'absence' is a general term, and absences might be due not to illness but to dental appointments etc which are arranged differently by the two groups in the sample. (Working mothers might arrange appointments after school hours, whereas non-working mothers might take their children out of school for appointments.) Moreover, the two groups of children may not be similar in terms of age, social background etc, making comparison less useful.

The reasons why the questions are important is that you need to be sure the information was gathered objectively and that the results have not been distorted in the interests of a particular pressure group.

C   The same kind of questions should be asked here. In the second survey, it would be very important to know if the intake of the schools surveyed is similar, to ensure that 'like is being compared with like'.

15 Criticising statistics

Before students read the reactions in the speech bubbles, you could ask '*How do you think local teenagers felt when they saw this written about them? Pleased? Angry? What do you think they said?*'

Elicit some reactions expressing indignation and a refusal to believe the results. Chorus drill appropriate responses, including those in the Student's Book. Check that students sound annoyed and disbelieving, before asking them to practise in pairs with the information in exercise 14.

16 Young lives: Good or bad?

Students work in pairs to analyse the statements about teenagers.

ANSWERS

Statements giving a positive impression are: 2, 3, 6, 7, 10.

Statements giving a negative impression are: 1, 4, 5, 8, 9.

You could encourage students to think about the situation in their own country(ies) by asking:

'Are teenagers in your country less materialistic than the ones in the survey?'
'Are they more community-minded than the teenagers in the survey?'
'Where do teenagers you know get their spending money from?'

17 Rewriting in a more formal style

The aim of this exercise is to consolidate work done in earlier units about appropriateness of style, tone and register. The letter, which is too informal for its purpose, could be analysed in small groups. It is packed with inappropriate expressions (*hopping mad, You too, I bet, Talk about …, dead worried* etc), so all the students should be able to find some.

After they have analysed the letter in pairs, ask students *'When would you write a letter in this style?'*, eliciting something along the lines of 'when you write to a friend, or to a college newsletter if the normal tone of the newsletter is very student-centred and informal.'

You could ask a student to come to the board and write up examples of inappropriate language under the headings given.

Before students attempt to rewrite the letter, suggest some phrases they could use to refer to the statistical information given in the original, e.g.

With regard to/With reference to the comment about …
I disagree with/object to the comment that …

MODEL ANSWER

A copy of the model letter could be circulated to students for comparison with their own attempts.

Dear Sir,

I am a pupil at a local comprehensive school. I have just read your report 'Young Lives Shock!' and I feel most annoyed about the way it describes teenagers. We are not 'unconcerned about employment'. My friends and I are very worried about the chances of getting a job in a town with high unemployment like this one.

I also disagree with your report's suggestion that 'teenagers value their spare-time jobs more than their studies'. Like the teenagers in the survey, I too have a part-time job to earn extra spending money. As my father is a single parent, he is unable to afford to buy me the trainers or CDs I would like. I work in a café twice a week after school. It does make it hard to concentrate at school the next day, but I do extra homework to catch up.

With regard to the comment 'the youth of today show a strong preference for the company of their peer group over that which their parents can offer', I think it is more natural to want to spend time with friends of your own age than to stay at home with your parents. However, I would like to point out that teenagers respect their parents more than any other adults.

I would be most interested in hearing the responses of the other readers to this survey.

Yours faithfully,

Paul Stanton

INTERNATIONAL OVERVIEW

As always, check students' basic understanding of the table by asking such questions as *'What does the table show us?'* and also making sure they have grasped the meaning of tertiary (post-secondary) education or training.

Interesting discussion points arising from the table to select for your class include:

- What is the right age to leave school to study at college and/or start a training course?
- Is it better to study/train for a job in your own country or overseas?
- What kinds of jobs should people be trained to do if they are really to help their country progress?
- Is tertiary education open to anyone who wants it in your country? If it is not, should learning facilities be increased so that more people can study?
- Tertiary education is very expensive to develop. How can it be funded?

Job stereotypes

18 Pre-listening discussion

The pre-listening activity focuses on the topic of shopping from a consumer's point of view. To help students decide on how they would improve shops, you could explore common pet hates about shopping, e.g. queuing for service, pushy/indifferent /ignorant salespeople, difficulty in getting the goods you want/refunds, etc.

19 Predicting content

Students predict the content of the personnel officer's talk before listening. Make sure they understand the concept of a personnel officer, as it will not be common in all cultures. Personnel officers are employed in many large organisations. They are involved in recruitment and interviewing, but often their key function is staff welfare and helping staff do their jobs more effectively.

POSSIBLE ANSWERS

The most likely personnel functions are Suggesting … and Disciplining … (covered in the talk), and Helping … and Encouraging … .

20 Vocabulary check

ANSWERS

personal sales targets: levels of sales which individuals are aiming to achieve
influential: able to influence or have an effect
wide spectrum: a broad range

21 Listening for gist / 22 Detailed listening

 As always, allow students to listen first for general meaning and then for specific information. Remind them that in the exam their listening comprehension answers can be short but must be clear and unambiguous.

ANSWERS

1   Product knowledge, how to sell, display of goods.
2   They want to sack or discipline them.
3   She persuades managers to analyse the skills needed for the job and to see that a wide range of people can have those skills.
4   When a store's sales have fallen because of a change in circumstances (a rival store has opened up, or people are moving away from the area).
5   She has a good relationship, based on persuasion and advice.

TAPESCRIPT

Listen to the recording. Which of the points that you ticked are mentioned?

What I do is I visit electrical stores in the high streets up and down the country. I'm really trying to advise the managers on staffing so that, you know, they can get the best out of their staff.

One common problem is er … well, for example, say a sales assistant is not meeting personal sales targets. Their figures are, you know, a bit … iffy. Managers are wondering, like, are they up to the job, should they get the sack or not? I suggest how about offering the

assistant more training and more development. Of course, training … it would have to be in a specific area. I mean, we get a sales assistant who knows everything about hi-fi but nothing about the white goods like fridges and dishwashers we sell. So they have a gap where product knowledge is concerned. And this can be rectified if they go on a training course. Sometimes we let them take a microwave or camera home so that they can get familiar with it in their own time. On the other hand, a few, er …, quite a few, sales assistants need training in exactly how to sell. Selling involves opening the sale and actually closing the sale to make sure the transaction is complete – clinching the deal, if you like.

Another common gap is display. In a shop, goods should be displayed so they appeal to the customer, they're easy to find, er …, well there's no point in creating confusion, is there? An assistant may be sent on a course to train them in how to set out the goods logically, taking into account the height, colour, …

It's funny, but the most frustrating aspect of my job is that managers want very quick results. Well, who wouldn't want their shop to be the best? But they want to sack people or discipline them rather than invest more in training and keep people. Managers find it hard to accept that the personnel officer is influential. When it comes to recruiting staff, it's usually the case that managers want people just like themselves – same background, all that – well, when what you actually need are the skills and attributes for the job. I get managers to see that, well, people from a wide spectrum can meet the needs of the job. Er, yeah, I'd say I … I feel most satisfied when I've persuaded managers to take on people who, er, don't fit the norm.

Sometimes, and this is in its way a much more serious thing, the store's sales are falling too. If a rival store has opened up, it'll be taking our custom or maybe the population in the area is declining – er, it's just that people are moving away. In this case, it's no good projecting sales by looking at the figures of the previous year. I'd help them project new targets, more, er, realistic targets, taking these factors into account. I try to get on well with the managers. They have to feel they've got the power. After all, you know, they do work hard and it can be a bit of a treadmill. I never make them do anything – if it went wrong, they'd blame me. I can influence but not, well … at the end of the day, they've got to feel the decisions come from them.

23 Post-listening discussion

The aim of the discussion is to explore stereotyping. The personnel officer says that sales managers want to employ people who are like themselves. It will be interesting to hear students' perceptions of the kind of person she has in mind.

You could now write the occupation *rock star* on the board and ask students '*How would you describe a typical rock star?*', perhaps inviting one of them to draw a caricature on the board. Elicit ideas about appearance, lifestyle, clothes, spare-time interests etc. Students could then discuss the other occupations in pairs.

Ask for feedback on the group discussion which follows. Students will probably not have any particular difficulty in distinguishing between the popular stereotypes and reality, but you could ask

'Are all librarians serious/do they all wear glasses/are they all fond of reading?', for example.

To help students focus on whether stereotypes are a good or bad thing, you could ask *'Are school or college leavers put off some occupations by stereotyping? How far have you found stereotypes to be true to life? Who do you know who doesn't fit the stereotype for their occupation?'*

24 Common work-related expressions

ANSWERS

1 talk about work
2 an ambitious person
3 money given when he retired
4 not working
5 person who does menial jobs at work
6 have control over how and when I work
7 a high achieving person
8 manual workers, officer workers

25 Pronunciation: Linking sounds

Tell students that if a word ends with a consonant sound, it will link with the next word if that word begins with a vowel sound. Ask them to listen to you reading the advert, so that they can hear how some words are pronounced distinctly and others 'run into' the next word. Before they practise reading the advert aloud, remind them that, as always, pronunciation is part of meaning – for the meaning to be conveyed clearly, the pronunciation must be satisfactory too.

HEADLIGHTS HAIRDRESSING: ANSWERS

Career‿opportunities

Learn‿in‿a

got‿energy and‿enthusiasm

Contact‿Isabel

26 Writing a job advert

POSSIBLE ANSWER

GENERAL‿ASSISTANT FOR LABORATORY

Saturday help needed to wash glassware, sweep‿up and generally tidy the laboratory. £4 per‿hour plus travel‿expenses.

Contact‿Amy Jones 013452–78642

Monitor the pairs as they read to each other, and correct any faulty pronunciation.

Recruitment with a difference

27 Pre-reading task

The reading text which follows is of a similar length and difficulty to Paper 2, Part 1, exercise 3. It is about a fast-food restaurant which employs deaf and mute staff. The text is based on an interview with the restaurant manager, who relates how his feelings of trepidation changed to enthusiasm when he realised how smoothly the system worked and all the benefits it offered to the disabled employees.

A Possible advantages of fast-food restaurants are:

- good when you are in a hurry
- clean, hygienic surroundings
- informal – you can go alone or with a group of friends
- relatively inexpensive
- consistent quality of food
- familiar menu wherever you are.

B Encourage students to write open questions, e.g.

Why did you decide to employ deaf and mute staff?
How do the staff communicate with customers?
What roles do the staff have in the restaurant?
What training do they have?
How do hearing people communicate with them?
What difficulties have you had?
How do customers react?
How successful has it been?

28 Vocabulary check

hearing impairment: reduction in ability to hear (You could highlight the use of *im-* as a prefix in words such as *impatience*, *impossible*, *impractical*, *immature*, *impassable*, all suggesting a lack or reduction of something.)
recruiting: finding new employees
agile: quick in movement
criteria: standards for judging/deciding something
mentor: more experienced person who inspires and advises

29 Reading for gist

Students should enjoy finding answers to the questions they wrote.

30 Comprehension check

ANSWERS

1 The management were aware of the large numbers of deaf and dumb people in society and felt they had a duty to help them.
2 They used the same criteria as when they select hearing applicants.
3 In previous jobs the employees felt isolated but here they feel normal, which is very positive for them.
4 They become more energetic and better tempered.

5 Any two of: learned basic sign language; changed his attitudes towards disabled people; gained a sense of personal fulfilment because he has made a difference to people's lives.

31 Post-reading discussion

A Discuss students' reactions to the idea of employing people with disabilities in other companies. You could ask, for example, '*Could a blind person be a teacher? What special aids might they need?*'

You could relate the concept of sign language to the importance of general body language in conveying meaning, asking students to explore how we communicate through facial expressions, gestures, movement, posture etc, and also how opinions of people are formed based on their body language.

B When students discuss the contrasting rewards and stresses of people-orientated jobs and product-orientated jobs, they will be generalising to some extent. It may be quite a difficult, abstract concept for those who have not had employment experience. Prompt them if necessary to elicit ideas along these lines:

'In a people-orientated job, you have to learn to cope with many different kinds of personalities and expectations. They may have more needs than you can satisfy, and so the work might feel outside your control at times. You can gain rewards through a feeling of being valued and respected by those people on whose behalf you work.

In a product-orientated job, you have the satisfaction of producing something that you can, in a sense, stand back and admire at the end of the day. On the other hand, the work can be more monotonous as it does not have the unpredictable element people-orientated jobs bring.'

C It will be interesting to hear students' views on 'mentoring'. You could develop the idea to include mentors in the family or social sphere, such as aunts and uncles who befriend younger relatives who need someone to confide in, and who feel isolated in their immediate family.

32 Vocabulary study

Students can work in pairs for this exercise.

ANSWERS

A manic, hyperactive, energetic, lazy/indolent, bone idle

B loving, affectionate, supportive, friendly, indifferent, cold, critical

C equable

33 Similes

Ask students to read their similes aloud.

POSSIBLE ANSWERS

1 an oven
2 ice
3 it hadn't been cleaned for years
4 she had won the lottery
5 being in prison
6 life wasn't worth living
7 talking to a brick wall

34 Spelling: ...*able* or ...*ible*?

Before students start the spelling exercise, you could write up *preventable* and *responsible* and highlight the endings. Then you could elicit other words with these endings. Unfortunately, there are no clear and simple rules for the spelling patterns, so remind students of the importance of learning the endings by heart. *Responsible* is commonly misspelt in the exam.

ANSWERS

A **1** available
2 invisible
3 curable
4 responsible
5 incredible
6 sensible
7 reliable
8 advisable
9 inaccessible
10 irritable

B **1** washable
2 inedible
3 digestible
4 desirable
5 approachable
6 excitable
7 bearable
8 incomprehensible

35 Phrasal verbs

ANSWERS

1 get by
2 carry out
3 turn down
4 leave anyone out
5 drawn up

36 'Eye' idioms

ANSWERS

An *eye-opening* experience is one which makes you realise things for the first time.

1h **2**g **3**f **4**a **5**c **6**e **7**b **8**d

Preparing for work

37 How well does school prepare you for work?

A   Students may well not have a specific idea of their future career, but you could invite them to think of the positive ways school is preparing them, in general, to be successful in employment. Their ideas could range across the subjects of the curriculum, e.g. good communication skills and being numerate are essential for work in most areas, computer literacy is useful as the use of computers in firms increases, an understanding of science helps you use technical equipment safely, etc. Moreover, personal qualities which are needed at work such as team leadership, being a good team player, creativity and imagination are developed at school by many subjects including sport, art and extra-curricular activities.

B   Holding a position of responsibility at school also develops personal qualities. Encourage students to identify strengths which they have gained, e.g. confidence, good organisational skills, empathy, self-discipline.

38 Before you read

The pre-reading task leads into a reading and writing exercise.

Before students begin the task, it's useful to clarify the concept of 'Head Prefect', as not everyone will be familiar with this position, especially if their school does not have prefects. Explain that it's a position filled by a pupil in the final year of school who has shown outstanding qualities of leadership, etc. A head prefect may be elected by the pupils or chosen by the teachers. He/she does such things as negotiate with teachers over matters of discipline and pupil grievances, and is trusted by the teachers to act as an 'ambassador' to the other pupils, explaining the teachers' point of view over unpopular rules etc.

You could also discuss the disadvantages of the prefect/head prefect system. It is sometimes thought to encourage resentment and hostility among pupils and has been scrapped in some UK schools for this reason.

39 Reading, analysing and writing

The newsletter article by Luke is written in the mature style which would earn the highest marks in the exam.

It's a good idea to introduce the completion task by explaining that the exam is looking for a 'sustained' quality of writing. An article which begins well but tails off will not gain the highest marks. As always, students need to give attention to the whole of the text they produce.

Students should work together to decide how the letter could end and then complete the text.

MODEL ANSWER

Matthew is the best candidate and would be an ideal Head Prefect. He has good all-round skills and he has proved his ability to work for the school and get on with all kinds of pupils. I would definitely trust him to represent our point of view to the teachers.

40 Comparing two styles

Students should have no difficulty in recognising the immaturity of Kirsty's style. You could ask *'Which article carries more authority/would influence you more? Why?'*

A suitable answer would be something like:

'The short, simple sentences, bald tone, abrupt register and lack of organisation make the article much less authoritative than that written by Luke.'

41 Rewriting in a more mature style

Rewriting Kirsty's article is quite challenging, and you may like to invite students to work on various possible drafts in groups until they have produced a draft everyone is satisfied with. Remind them that Luke's article should give them some ideas of structures etc.

MODEL ANSWER

HEAD PREFECT ELECTIONS

My personal choice for Head Prefect is Nicola Wilson. She has worked extremely hard for all of us and her behaviour is a shining example to the rest of the pupils.

Do you remember how many of us were being bullied and afraid to come to school? She tackled this problem very effectively and the bullying is no longer an issue. It was also Nicola's idea to start a 'Welcome Day' for new pupils, which has really helped new students integrate quickly and happily.

The fact that we have a brilliant social club is due to Nicola's hard work too. She worked round the clock to set one up. We now have a wonderful place to meet our friends and unwind after school.

She also negotiates confidently with teachers. Her discussions with the headteacher led to the girls being given permission to wear trousers in winter, which is much more comfortable for us and something we had wanted for a long time.

Her work visiting patients at our local hospital who do not normally receive visitors has developed her understanding of people's needs. This is a great asset in a big, mixed comprehensive like this one.

Nicola is not as egotistical as many of the prefects, and I know I speak for many of us when I say 'Vote for Nicola'. She is trustworthy, hardworking and, what is more, likeable!

42 Brainstorming

Unemployment may not be a big problem for your students in their particular situations. Nevertheless, the exam is looking for an ability to discuss issues of global concern. This exercise is a good opportunity for students to think about the problem of unemployment in their own country. As always, encourage them to give local examples, as the exam rewards the ability to adapt a composition question to a local situation. If you have a multicultural class, it's nice to share ideas about the various economies students come from.

Asking students to read a newspaper article or watch a TV programme about unemployment a day or two before you intend to cover the topic will focus on some of the issues and give them food for thought. Alternatively, they could interview their parents or other adults they have contact with about the causes and remedies of unemployment.

Before they begin brainstorming, ask students to study the photograph. (A 'Job Centre' in Britain is a government office where local job vacancies are advertised. Most towns have one.)

You could ask questions such as:
'Do you think the men have jobs to go to?
What are they doing?
How do you think they are going to spend the rest of the day?
How do you think they are feeling?'

Encourage students to write down all their ideas during the brainstorming, no matter how mad they seem!

43 Reading a model letter

The model letter follows on from the discussion about unemployment. It raises some ideas which could be followed up after the reading, e.g. Should unemployed people receive 'dole' (welfare payments to provide the necessities of life)? What way of life do unemployed people in your country have? Why might some people genuinely prefer unemployment to having a job?

ANSWERS

1 Young people need effective careers guidance.
2 A mentoring scheme would be helpful.
3 A partnership of local firms and schools could be set up to teach computer skills.
4 We are aware of the personal effects of unemployment.

44 Analysing the letter

ANSWERS

Defining clauses

Para 1: *I read your report which suggested …*
Para 2: *schools should start a 'mentoring scheme' which would match pupils …*
Para 3: *to develop training schemes which would enable us …*

Comparative structures

Para 2: *school leavers need much more detailed careers guidance*

Idioms

Para 1: *on the dole*
Para 2: *an eye-opener*
Para 4: *in the same boat*

Similes

Para 5: *like a high wall you have to climb over*

Linking devices

Para 2: *Moreover*
Para 3: *Furthermore, whereas*
Para 4: *I would also like to add that …*

Opening sentence

I do not usually write to newspapers but …

Conclusion

Young people need all the help they can get, not criticism.

Style and register

The overall impression is formal, which is appropriate for a letter to a newspaper.

45 Writing a letter of reply

Remind students that the letter of reply should be formal but not excessively so. IGCSE candidates are fond of language such as 'I am honoured that you have read my letter', which is too formal. The right tone should be that of two equals sharing views.

46 Choosing appropriate vocabulary

The aim of this exercise is to show that vocabulary and structures act as 'triggers', immediately conveying the right meaning. Exam marking is to some extent impressionistic, so it's essential that students convey the right impression as quickly as possible.

You may like to reinforce the message about rubric error because, sadly, some candidates do continue to misinterpret questions. Question interpretation is a tricky area because the questions nearly always have some cultural content. Problems arise because the interpretation is too literal, or because candidates are put off by the artificiality of the exercise and can't think into the situation quickly enough.

Sometimes misinterpretation appears deliberate: candidates try to stretch the definition of the task to exploit previously prepared material. The marks they receive will depend on the relevance of what they write. However, there's the possibility of getting no marks at all if the composition is completely off the point.

If you think your students need more familiarity with interpreting question topics, you could write up some essay questions which would not be set in the exam because they are clearly much too culturally loaded (about a church jumble sale, for example) or would be to the advantage of candidates with prior knowledge (the functions of the heart, or burial rites in ancient Egypt, for instance). Elicit from students what makes these questions unacceptable for the IGCSE exam. Ask them to suggest more likely areas for question setting, e.g. topics and themes of general/young people's interest.

ANSWERS

Question 1
budget deficit
sales figures
dawdled
indifferent
strolled
share prices

Question 2
sarcastic
bitterly disappointed
repelled
aggrieved
isolated
cast down
disenchanted
subdued
forsaken
irritated

Question 3
hostile
poison pen letter
sick and tired
deeply depressed
ill at ease
disgusted
unjust
macabre
outraged
terrified
contemptuous

47 Timed writing

Timed writing is important because students find concentrating their thoughts and producing coherent compositions in a short space of time very challenging. Let them have more classroom practice on other questions if necessary.

Allow students to read their compositions aloud either to their group or in pairs. Emphasise the value of honest but constructive criticism. Insist that each 'listener' finds two positive things to say about the compositions before suggesting criticisms and positive ways the writing could be improved.

Exam-format questions

Listening

 This listening exercise is typical of Paper 4, Part 1, in which candidates answer questions on six short listening texts, which they hear twice. At the Core level (Paper 3), three of the six texts and questions are the same as those on Paper 4.

ANSWERS

1 Friday morning
2 computer skills
3 patience and stamina
4 visit the place first
5 help your grandfather at the petrol station so that he can rest more.
6 Rome

TAPESCRIPT

For questions 1-6 you will hear a series of short sentences. Answer each question as briefly as possible. Full sentences are not required. You will hear each question twice.

1 Maria is ringing up to change the time and date of a job interview. What alternative is she offered?

   'You said the interview was Tuesday at 4 p.m. and that's when you're seeing the specialist? Yes, well if you think you can get here on Friday morning, we can fit you in then.'

2 You are listening to the radio when you hear the following advertisement. What training course is available?

   'Want to improve your job opportunities? You can take a computer skills course at times to suit you. Ring us at any time to make an appointment.'

3 Your class is listening to a careers talk for school-leavers. What two personal qualities are needed to enter training schemes for the police force?

   'Well, many of you will be surprised that, apart from a good standard of general education, no special qualifications are needed for our basic entry scheme. More important, in fact, are patience and stamina, as the hours are often long and the work is demanding.'

4 A friend tells you she wants to do voluntary work. What advice has she received?

   'I told the headteacher I wanted to help at the children's clinic. She agreed it would be very good experience for me, and she encourages us all to do something for the community. But she felt I should visit the place first – so I've decided to ring the clinic and ask if I can visit next week.'

5 You are visiting your grandmother. What does she want you to do, and why?

   'Grandad wanted me to ask you something. Now the exams are over, do you think you could find time to help him run the petrol station? It would mean grandad could rest more, and he'll be able to pay you a bit, too.'

6 A cousin phones to say he will be unable to come to a family celebration. Where will he go instead?

'I'm really sorry – I won't be able to make it. Do give my love to everyone. I've just received a letter saying I've been accepted onto a trainee pilot course. You know I've always wanted to fly, so I'm off to Rome to meet all the other trainees.'

WIDER PRACTICE

1 The charts below provide extra practice in comprehension and interpretation of visual data. They also provide a basis for discussing with students topics such as long working hours, job insecurity, jobs and family life, and work-related stress. These are culturally-loaded areas, so students from different countries might have quite opposing views.

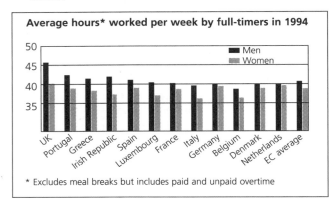

Average hours* worked per week by full-timers in 1994

* Excludes meal breaks but includes paid and unpaid overtime

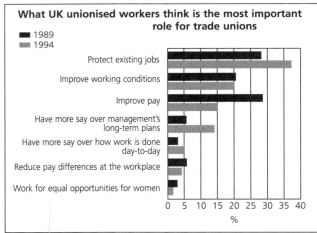

What UK unionised workers think is the most important role for trade unions

2 You could ask students to bring in examples of articles presenting statistical information in a way which, in their opinion, distorts the truth. They could argue their case in their groups.

3 Students might like to devise a questionnaire to use with local firms to find out more about their employment policies, e.g. working conditions and pay, health and safety, equal opportunity issues, recruitment, training schemes. Alternatively, a real live personnel officer or senior member of a firm could be invited to talk about their approach to employment. This could be done in conjunction with a careers lesson, if appropriate.

4 Students could beat the examiners at their own game by devising exam-style questions and marking schemes. You could choose a number of reading items and divide the class into groups, each with a separate reading text. One group could devise true/false questions, another a guided notetaking, another short-answer comprehension questions, and so on. The groups could decide on the marking scheme and ask the other groups to take the test, which they could later mark according to the mark scheme. This should generate some interesting discussion such as whether answers are 'close enough' to the mark scheme to be acceptable.

5 It's nice to reduce exam fever by means of the following exercise, which generates lots of laughs and informal conversation.

Students write sentence completions on three pieces of paper:

- *The way I relax during exams is …*
- *The best way I find to revise is …*
- *The way I'm going to treat myself when the exams are over is …*

Ask students not to write their names. The papers are then dropped into a box and shuffled, and each student selects one from the box. They walk around the room, stopping and asking each other open questions such as '*How do you relax during exams?*' until they find the person who wrote the original. They share their views and then choose another piece of paper.